# SOUTHERN KETO
## Beyond the Basics

More of the Easy Comfort Food You Love

## Natasha Newton

VICTORY BELT PUBLISHING

Las Vegas

*To all the fans of* Southern Keto, *this is for you.*
*Without your continued support and encouragement to write*
*another book, this wouldn't have been possible. Thank you!*

First Published in 2021 by Victory Belt Publishing Inc.

ISBN-13: 978-1-628603-95-8

The author is not a licensed practitioner, physician, or medical professional and offers no medical diagnoses, treatments, suggestions, or counseling. The information presented herein has not been evaluated by the U.S. Food and Drug Administration, and it is not intended to diagnose, treat, cure, or prevent any disease. Full medical clearance from a licensed physician should be obtained before beginning or modifying any diet, exercise, or lifestyle program, and physicians should be informed of all nutritional changes.

The author/owner claims no responsibility to any person or entity for any liability, loss, or damage caused or alleged to be caused directly or indirectly as a result of the use, application, or interpretation of the information presented herein.

Author photos by Lisa Presnell

Cover photo and photos on pages 42, 44, 69, 72, 97, 104, 126, 169, 188, 212, 251, 264, and 274 by Justin-Aaron Velasco and Kat Lannom

Food styling for cover photo and photos on pages 42, 44, 69, 72, 97, 104, 126, 169, 188, 212, 251, 264, and 274 by Marcella Capasso

Interior design and illustrations by Justin-Aaron Velasco and Kat Lannom

Printed in Canada

TC 0121

# ❋ Contents ❋

# ❋ Introduction ❋

Yay, y'all! Welcome back! I'm so glad you came. Come on in and have a seat at my table. I'd never dreamed that *Southern Keto* would make the impact that it has; I just hoped to write a good cookbook that would help a few people on the journey. It's been so exciting to see that the book has reached so many of you around the world and to hear the many different ways it has touched your lives. Some of you loved the new and easy recipes; some of you were thrilled that your picky kids or other non-keto family members enjoyed the food; some of you were just happy to see that the recipes use everyday ingredients that can be found at the grocery store. And then there were some of you who connected with my story as if it were your own.

Since many of you have asked for and encouraged me to write another book, I am beyond grateful for this opportunity to present to you *Southern Keto: Beyond the Basics*. It is filled with more easy recipes for the Southern comfort foods you love. It's my hope that you'll find in this book many new favorites that you and your family will enjoy for years to come!

Even though Southern food is most often equated with comfort food and soul food, we know that all regional cuisines have their forms of comfort food and that we all share the same feeling of comfort that comes from making and sharing meals. In my case, when I think of comfort food, I'm transported back in time to my grandma Ida Mae's kitchen. Ida Mae was a fabulous cook, and I loved watching her cook and spending time with her. However, as wonderful as her food was, I now know it is the love and care she put into cooking for her family and the time we spent sharing meals together that bring back the warm memories. It's the same kind of love and care that I hope my family and friends feel when I cook for them; it's the same Southern hospitality that I hope you experience as you make the recipes from both *Southern Keto* books. Comfort food transcends our regions and backgrounds; it brings us together. This book includes comfort food recipes beyond the basic, classic Southern dishes for this reason.

# The Journey Goes On

It's been almost two years since the release of *Southern Keto.* These years have been amazing, challenging, and filled with many emotions that can't be put into words. As I am finishing up this book in the autumn of 2020, we are in a pandemic. These are unprecedented times. None of us could have foreseen the events that have unfolded around the world over the last several months. And as secure as I feel in my way of eating, which has become a lifestyle for me these past few years, I have been tested. I have dealt with emotions that blindsided me. As someone with a history of emotional eating, I've found myself struggling in ways I never thought I would again. I'm fighting this just like everyone else.

All of this has reminded me once again that life is an ongoing journey, that we must not give up or give in amidst hard times or setbacks, and that things won't always be like this—they'll get better! I'm sharing this because sometimes you look around and think everyone else is handling things better than you. These thoughts can bring you down. The truth is that you are not alone; it's been a hard year for everyone. No matter how far you feel like you've been set back, you can make a comeback. There are ups and downs along this journey, and this is why building a solid foundation is so important. I've always loved the quote: "It's hard to beat a person who never gives up." And over the past six years, my motto has been to never give up. I know it sounds cliché—it's the kind of quote you see on T-shirts—but there's power in this mindset. Yes, the journey gets hard at times. Yes, there are days when I feel defeated. But I don't stop trying. It only took me forty-six years to figure these things out!

It's important also to realize that there's so much more to this journey than weight loss (although you couldn't have convinced me of this years ago!). I used to think that if I could just be a certain size or achieve a certain level of success, then I would be happy. Boy, was I wrong! These things are great, but there are many layers to our journey. Emotions are more complex than we may realize, and we need to keep in mind that mental health is just as crucial to our overall well-being as physical health.

# Where It All Started

You see, some days I still feel like that little girl I used to be who was a yo-yo dieter and binge eater. Food obsession and unhealthy thinking and eating patterns started at a very young age for me. I was just a kid; I didn't care about losing weight. And even though my parents tried to keep our kitchen stocked with what they believed was healthy food, when they weren't looking, I would eat everything I could get my hands on. At nine years old, I was placed on my first medically supervised diet. This was back in the eighties when FAT WAS THE ENEMY. The food was, of course, boring. Cue the rice cakes! These plain, dry, cardboard-like rice cakes would taste good to me only with a thick slather

of peanut butter on them. But that was a big no-no because peanut butter is, well, "fattening." Oh, and let's not forget the SnackWell's cookies. I was eating a whole box of these "fat-free" cookies and wondering why this diet wasn't working! These foods were thought to be healthier, but they actually contained a lot of sugar, which only intensified my food cravings. Needless to say, I didn't lose any weight on that diet program.

You may think I probably had a bad childhood or some sort of trauma that triggered my unhealthy eating patterns. The truth is I didn't. I am grateful to be able to say that I had loving and supportive parents. It's just that I always struggled with food addiction, which is so hard for me to admit and may seem ridiculous to people who have never had that struggle. People will say, "Why don't you just do moderation in everything?" And my response to that is always, "Don't you think I would if it were that easy?!" (This, by the way, is such a tone-deaf attitude to have when what we need is more empathy for the millions of people who struggle with food addiction and binge eating disorders. These people are not lazy and lacking self-control; they're simply overpowered by the effects of sugar on the brain! Instead of condemning them, we need to end the stigma and encourage people to see that there is hope!)

The struggle continued into my teen years. It was a tough time of my life when I didn't feel like I fit in. I loved fashion, but there weren't many options for me. I remember wanting Jordache jeans so badly but ended up getting a pair of boys' husky jeans because they were the only ones that fit. I had extremely low self-esteem. Body positivity was unheard of back then; loving yourself the way you are was never spoken of, either. In fact, many times I was told I had a pretty face and that if I just lost a little weight... I don't remember having childhood dreams or ambitions; I simply didn't think I had anything to offer or was capable of doing anything significant. It's incredibly sad to me now to have realized that I felt that way only because of my size!

My first significant weight loss came from taking diet pills at age eighteen. I didn't care if it was dangerous; I was desperate to lose weight and finally fit in and be "normal." I thought I had literally found the "magic pill" because the medication made it easy for me to go without food. However, when I did eat, I would be eating a lot of sugar and carbs, like giant bowls of sugary fat-free cereal with skim milk (because it was—you guessed it—fat free). Even though I lost some weight, I couldn't keep it off, and my cravings would be as intense as ever. Dieting became my lifestyle. I would try every diet and pill imaginable, while my weight went up and down and up and down. It was a vicious cycle.

After many years of dieting, I topped out at 309 pounds—at least that was the last number I saw on the scale before I stopped weighing myself. I now wore the largest size offered at Lane Bryant and was starting to order from plus-size stores that sold larger sizes. I felt very uncomfortable and embarrassed. I was depressed, which led to more emotional eating. Scared and feeling like I was reaching the point of no return, I went on yet another diet and lost 50 pounds before I got pregnant with my youngest. After that pregnancy, I continued with binge eating followed by many more diets, losing and gaining 50 to over 100 pounds multiple times.

In 2004, at age twenty-nine, I lost a lot of weight again. Then life threw me a curveball: I became very sick and was diagnosed with a moderate to severe case of Crohn's disease. After that fateful call from the doctor, "no cure" was all my mind kept repeating over and over. It was a very isolated, lonely time in my life. I had two small children to take care of; my husband worked hard; and we had no family nearby. As the following decade became a blur of sickness, flares, hospitalizations, and surgeries, I turned to my biggest comfort: food.

## How I Found Keto

Just when I had all but given up on ever losing weight again, I started noticing stories about keto that had popped up on social media through hashtags like #keto and #lowcarb. I read all the wonderful testimonies of people losing weight and getting healthy, and I saw lots of before-and-after pictures. Well, we all love a good before-and-after, don't we? I had many of those myself. However, it wasn't the pictures that made me want to try keto; it was what the people in those pictures were saying that intrigued me. They said they weren't hungry on keto. They *weren't hungry*? They weren't hungry and they *enjoyed the food*? I was always hungry when I was on a diet. I thought it was mandatory to feel deprived!

After throwing myself into research and reading everything I could about keto, I decided to give it a try even though I had my doubts since I had tried everything else. I lost 20 pounds rather quickly afterward, which I thought was great. However, I treated keto as just another diet, which means I didn't think or care about mindset, lifestyle, growth, or changing my relationship with food. Sure enough and soon enough, my old habits and eating patterns reemerged, and I gained back those twenty pounds. Even so, keto wasn't far from my mind. In fact, I started missing it. I remember thinking to myself: *Well, this is weird. How can I miss a diet?* What really happened was that I missed how I felt when I was eating keto. I had a nagging feeling that if I didn't go back to eating that way, I was missing out on possibly the only thing that would ever work for me.

So I recommitted, starting back with a new mission—not only to look better but also to feel better. I really wanted to make it a lifestyle, and I did. It didn't happen overnight, though; I still had plenty of ups and downs. But the more consistent I became, the more natural it felt. Eventually, everything changed, and keto no longer felt like a diet to me. Not only did I lose weight, I also gained my life back. My health improved dramatically. Even though on paper I had been in remission from Crohn's disease even before keto, I still dealt with hard days and fatigue. However, after having stuck with keto consistently, I didn't have as many Crohn's-related symptoms. Even now, six years later, my energy and overall well-being are better than they've ever been. For that, my family and I are so thankful.

# Chapter 1

# ❧ Keto Basics ❦

What is keto? Contrary to what some people believe, there isn't one right way to do keto, and it isn't one-size-fits-all. Keto is not a specific food you eat; keto is a metabolic state. We eat low-carbohydrate, moderate-protein, and high-fat foods to get our bodies into the state of ketosis, where we use ketones rather than glucose for energy. The amount of carbs required will vary from person to person. Most people eat between 20 and 50 grams of net carbs per day.

People follow a ketogenic lifestyle for many different reasons. Weight loss is usually the top reason for most people, but the health benefits of keto extend far beyond that. Some have adopted keto as a way to control diabetes and seizures; some athletes eat this way to maximize their performance; some do it for the mental clarity that comes from a ketone-fueled diet. In my case, I originally started keto to lose weight. Along the way, however, I've come to realize that I feel so much better without sugar and refined carbs in my life.

# Reading Labels & Figuring Net Carbs

Net carbs are the carbs that are absorbed by the body. To calculate net carbs, subtract the fiber and sugar alcohols (if in food) from the total carbohydrates.

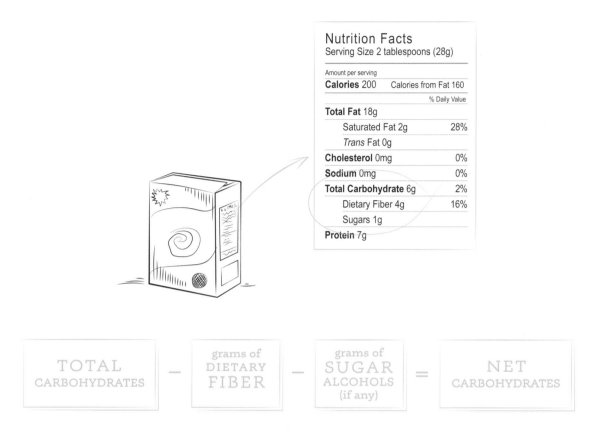

| Nutrition Facts | |
|---|---|
| Serving Size 2 tablespoons (28g) | |

| Amount per serving | |
|---|---|
| **Calories** 200 | Calories from Fat 160 |

| | % Daily Value |
|---|---|
| **Total Fat** 18g | |
| Saturated Fat 2g | 28% |
| *Trans* Fat 0g | |
| **Cholesterol** 0mg | 0% |
| **Sodium** 0mg | 0% |
| **Total Carbohydrate** 6g | 2% |
| Dietary Fiber 4g | 16% |
| Sugars 1g | |
| **Protein** 7g | |

| TOTAL CARBOHYDRATES | − | grams of DIETARY FIBER | − | grams of SUGAR ALCOHOLS (if any) | = | NET CARBOHYDRATES |
|---|---|---|---|---|---|---|

# Counting Macros Versus Intuitive Keto

There are three main macronutrients: fat, protein, and carbohydrates. The ideal daily ratio of macronutrients when eating keto appears to be 75 percent fat, 20 percent protein, and 5 percent carbohydrates. People have found that sticking to this ratio has helped them maintain a state of ketosis. Your mileage may vary, and I encourage you to find out the ratio that works best for you.

There are two approaches to monitoring macronutrients, one of which is known as "counting macros," and the other is intuitive keto. Counting macros involves a somewhat high level of precision in tracking how many grams of each macro you take in each day; an online keto calculator or apps such as MyFitnessPal and Carb Manager will come in handy for you. Intuitive keto (aka "lazy keto"), on the other hand, doesn't involve such close monitoring of all macros. People who use this approach typically keep a mental count of their daily net carbs, aiming for anywhere between 20 and 50 grams per day.

Experiment with both approaches to find out which fits your lifestyle and personality better. I have tried both and found that counting macros every day felt too restrictive and led to bingeing, whereas the freestyle approach of intuitive keto was what I could maintain in the long run. For me, it's about listening to as well as learning about my body and figuring out what makes me feel good. It has required patience and a willingness to learn what works for me and make changes as necessary. I eat normal-sized portions of allowable foods. I make conscious decisions about what to eat, and I eat until satisfied but not overly stuffed. Also, I no longer mindlessly snack. I've found that by doing this, my daily net carbs naturally fall within the range that works best in stabilizing my weight and maintaining my health.

Which method a person chooses greatly depends on their personality type. I know people who only have success on keto when they count macros. And some people truly enjoy that! Some people find that tracking their macros closely works in the beginning, and then transition to intuitive keto once they feel that they have obtained a good grasp of the keto lifestyle. You have to know yourself and your triggers. You've heard me say it before, and I'll say it again: keto is not one-size-fits-all. We are individuals and have individual needs. Use the method that works best for you. Set yourself up for success.

## Using Intermittent Fasting with Keto

I believe in keeping the keto lifestyle simple in order to maintain longevity, as I've found that the reason many people give up is because it seems too complicated. I can't tell you how many times I've heard naysayers say that keto just isn't sustainable. Some people like things a bit more complicated, they thrive on feeling challenged, and that is okay! Then there are those of us who need things to be a bit more streamlined. The key is knowing your patterns and finding what works for you.

However, keto is a tool. And as is the case with the various tools in life which you need to adjust along the way to make them work more effectively for your individual needs at different times, sometimes this tool keto needs to be tweaked or used in conjunction with another tool to get you to where you want to be. For me, that tool is intermittent fasting.

Fasting is not necessary to follow a ketogenic lifestyle. However, it's a tool which has been tremendously helpful in my keto journey. When I first started keto, I didn't know anything about fasting. Only after two years into keto did I hear about it and how, according to what people were saying, it seemed to help break weight loss stalls. With my weight loss having stalled for a year at that time, all this piqued my interest. Fasting seemed very difficult, however; I just couldn't imagine skipping any meals! But I was ready to try something new, so I decided to try a 16/8 fast, meaning I would eat all of my meals in an 8-hour window and fast for the remaining 16 hours each day. I stopped eating anything after 8 p.m. and resumed eating when my feeding window opened at noon the next day. The first two weeks were the hardest, and then it got easier from there. Now intermittent fasting is second nature for my body, and I'm no longer hungry in the mornings.

Many believe that intermittent fasting has more benefits than just weight loss. People have reported decreased inflammation, lower cholesterol and blood pressure, metabolic cellular repair, and increased cognitive brain function and memory. Intermittent fasting did break a weight loss stall for me, but the biggest difference I saw was in the way it made me feel. I have so much more energy when fasting; I am so much more productive during my fast; and I have the kind of mental clarity that I'd never experienced before (my favorite fasting benefit!). I've recently delved into the world of extended fasting to see what it would do to my body.

There are a few common types of fasts:

- 16/8—Fasting for 16 hours with an eating window of 8 hours each day. For me, a typical 16/8 fast begins at 6 p.m. and ends at 10 a.m.

- OMAD—Eating one meal a day

- Extended—Fasting for anywhere from 24 hours to many days

If you'd like to learn more about the science and health benefits of intermittent fasting, I recommend the book *The Complete Guide to Fasting* by Dr. Jason Fung and Jimmy Moore.

## Setting Yourself Up for Success

To be truthful, there was a time in my life when I was bitter about the hand that had been dealt to me; it all seemed so unfair. I wondered why I had to struggle with childhood obesity or why I got Crohn's disease and missed so much precious time with my kids when they were little. That was a dark time in my life when I was sick, tired, and filled with grief. And even though it wasn't in my nature to be negative and I knew I couldn't continue to live in bitterness, I couldn't help thinking how I had been cheated out of so many years of my life.

It's clear to me now that my attitude was setting me up for failure in every aspect of my life. I've come to see how I need to stop feeling sorry for myself and making excuses for my poor decisions. After six years of keto, I've learned a lot, and I'm still learning! I don't know it all. Even experts in their field are always learning and researching. I hope the following tips, which have helped me along my keto journey, will be helpful to you:

- **Be consistent. Consistency is the "secret."** Don't chase perfection. Being consistent is more important than perfection. If you go through hard times—and you will—just be consistent.

- **Take one day at a time.** It's okay to set goals, but don't overwhelm yourself by looking too far in the future.

- **Recognize self-sabotage.** If you know you have destructive tendencies, learn to recognize them. Find different coping mechanisms. This will take time.

- **Don't let a bad day derail you.** MOVE ON QUICKLY. If you let it, a bad day can turn into bad weeks and months.

- **Don't overcomplicate things!** You will only make yourself and those around you miserable, and you may even give up because you think this way of eating is too hard. I know because I was guilty of this habit. I made myself so unhappy trying to do everything perfectly.

- **Stop comparing yourself to others.** Don't compare your weight loss with anyone else's. This is your journey, and we all lose weight at our own pace. The same keto path will not work for everyone.

- **Your value is not based on a number on a scale or a clothing size.** It's okay to care about those things, but don't base your worth on them.

- **Try to focus on NSVs (non-scale victories).** How do you feel? How are your clothes fitting? Take pictures and measurements.

- **Have patience with yourself.** Your journey to health is not a race. There isn't a finish line. Decide to focus on a lifestyle that you can sustain, not diets.

Some days you will feel like you are on top of the world, unstoppable. Other days you will think: Why am I even doing this? Does it even matter? Yes, it matters. You matter. You are worthy. You are worth the fight. If you fall down, get back up and try again. Getting back up is the key. People often say that the road to success is paved with failure. That's so true in my life; my road to success has been paved with many failures, and I'm still on that road. I'm not perfect, but my mindset is healthier than ever.

# Stocking Your Keto Refrigerator, Freezer & Pantry

Being prepared is important to your success on the keto lifestyle. When you aren't prepared, it's easier to make less-than-ideal choices when you come home tired from a long day. I've prepared these grocery lists as a guide. Most of these items can easily be found at your local grocery store.

## Meats & Eggs

Bacon

Beef

Beef jerky (no sugar added)

Canned chicken breast

Canned salmon

Canned tuna

Chicken

Deli meats (uncured)

Eggs (I use the large size)

Fish

Hot dogs (uncured)

Lamb

Pepperoni (uncured)

Pork

Rotisserie chicken

Salami (uncured)

Sausage (uncured)

Shellfish

Turkey

## Dairy (full-fat)

Butter

Cheeses (hard and sliced)

Cottage cheese

Cream cheese

Heavy cream

Mascarpone cheese

Plain yogurt (full-fat, no sugar added)

Queso fresco

Sour cream

## High-Quality Fats & Oils

Avocado oil—has a high smoke point that makes it great for frying

Bacon drippings/grease—gives foods a lot of flavor

Butter—I use salted butter (I like the taste of Kerrygold), but if you prefer, you can use unsalted and adjust the amounts of salt in the recipes slightly

Coconut oil—has a high smoke point that makes it great for frying; you can use unrefined unflavored coconut oil if you don't like the taste of coconut

Extra-virgin olive oil—good for salad dressings and roasted veggies; I don't use it for frying because of its lower smoke point

Ghee—a good option for those who are sensitive to dairy; also has a high smoke point

MCT oil—medium-chain triglycerides (MCTs) are naturally occurring fatty acids in coconut oil; MCT oil is flavorless and can be added to coffee, smoothies, and salad dressings

Non-hydrogenated lard—has a neutral flavor and a high smoke point, making it good for frying

## Veggies (fresh & frozen)

Artichokes

Asparagus

Baby spinach

Banana peppers

Bell peppers

Broccoli

Brussels sprouts

Cabbage

Cauliflower

Celery

Collard greens

Cucumbers

Dill pickles

Eggplant

Garlic

Green beans

Green onions (aka scallions)

Hot peppers

Jalapeños

Kale

Lettuce

Mini sweet peppers

Mushrooms

Onions (red, white, and yellow)

Radishes

Rhubarb

Salad greens

Spaghetti squash

Swiss chard

Yellow squash

Zucchini

## Fruits & Berries

Avocados

Blackberries

Blueberries

Coconut (flakes and shredded; unsweetened)

Lemons

Limes

Olives

Raspberries

Strawberries

Tomatoes

## Ketogenic Seasonings

Blackening seasoning (see page 266 for a recipe)

Everything bagel seasoning

Herbs (fresh and dried)

Italian seasoning

Old Bay seasoning

Ranch seasoning (see page 267 for a recipe)

Salt (fine-grain and kosher-size)*

Seasoning salt

Spices

*I use kosher-size salt as a finishing salt on savory and sweet dishes and for rimming margarita glasses. For its superior flavor and health benefits, I use Real Salt's kosher-size sea salt; for a more affordable option, I recommend Diamond Crystal Kosher Salt.

## Baking Ingredients

Almond flour (finely ground blanched)

Baking powder (aluminum free)

Coconut flour

Flavor extracts and flavorings

Sugar-free chocolate chips (preferably Lily's brand)

Unflavored and unsweetened whey protein powder (aka whey protein isolate)

Xanthan gum

## Nuts, Seeds & Nut Butters

Almonds

Cashews

Chia seeds

Hazelnuts

Macadamia nuts

Natural almond butter (unsalted and unsweetened)

Natural peanut butter (unsalted and unsweetened)

Peanuts

Pecans

Pistachios

Pumpkin seeds, shelled

Sesame seeds

Sunflower seeds, shelled

Walnuts

## Sweeteners

Allulose

Erythritol

Pure monk fruit and monk fruit blended with erythritol

Stevia

Xylitol*

*Xylitol is keto-friendly, but I avoid it because it's dangerous if ingested by pets.

## Miscellaneous

Almond milk (unsweetened)

Bone broth (beef and chicken)

Cashew milk (unsweetened)

Coconut milk (full-fat)

Dill relish (no sugar added)

Ketchup (no sugar added)

Mayonnaise

Pork rinds

Salad dressings (full-fat, low-carb, and no sugar added)

Vegetable broth

# Where I Shop & What I Buy

When I first started keto years ago, keto-friendly options were limited. Now, you can go into just about any store and find many choices. However, use caution with products labeled "keto"; just because something is labeled as such doesn't mean it's great for your specific goals. Always check the ingredient labels and carb counts.

## Aldi

Apple cider vinegar *(organic)*

Avocado oil

Bacon

Biltong beef jerky

Butter

Cheese wraps

Coconut oil

Crepini egg wraps

Dilly Bites

Eggs

Everything bagel seasoning

Folios cheese wraps

Ghee

Heavy cream

Keto bread

Lunch meats *(uncured, nitrate-free)*

Meats *(fresh)*

Nuts and seeds

Parmesan crisps

Pepperoni

Pork rinds

Produce *(organic)*

Prosciutto

Riced cauliflower *(frozen)*

Salami

Sausage

Sour cream

Specialty cheeses *(hard and sliced)*

Stevia

Two Good Greek yogurt

## Costco

4505 chicharrones

Almond flour

Avocado oil

Avocados

Bacon

Berries

Birch Benders Keto Pancake & Waffle Mix

Bone broth

Bulk spices

Canned chicken breast

Canned sardines

Canned tuna

Cheeses

Chicken breasts

Chicken wings

Coconut oil

Coffee

Cold brew

Collagen peptides

Crepini egg wraps

Egg bites

Eggs

English cucumbers

Folios cheese wraps

Green nonstarchy vegetables

Ground beef

Guacamole *(in single-serving cups)*

Hamburgers *(precooked and frozen)*

Hard-boiled eggs

Heavy cream

Hot dogs *(uncured)*

Kerrygold butter

Keto snack mix

KetoPint ice cream bars

Kirkland protein bars

Lakanto keto granola

Lakanto monkfruit sweetener

Lump crab meat

Lunch meats *(uncured, nitrate-free)*

Marinara sauce

Mayonnaise

MCT oil

Moon Cheese

Natural almond butter

Nuts

Parm Crisps

Pimento cheese

Pork belly *(precooked)*

Pork chops

Pork panko

Pork ribs

Pork tenderloin

Ratio keto-friendly bars

Riced cauliflower *(fresh and frozen)*

Rotisserie chicken

Salsa *(organic)*

Sausages

Steaks

Tomatoes

Whisps cheese crisps

Wild Alaskan salmon

## Trader Joe's

Almond flour

Avocado oil

Avocados

Bacon

Bacon ends and pieces

Baking powder

Beef sticks

Bell peppers

Berries

Bone broth

Broccoli slaw

Broth *(organic)*

Brussels sprouts

Canned wild salmon

Cauliflower thins

Cheeses *(hard and sliced)*

Chia seeds

Coconut aminos

Coconut flour

Coconut milk

Coconut oil

Coconut oil spray

Dips and spreads

Extra-virgin olive oil

Flaxseed meal

Ghee

Green nonstarchy vegetables

Heavy cream

Jicama wraps

Kerrygold butter

Liquid stevia

Mascarpone cheese

Mini sweet peppers

Montezuma's Absolute Black chocolate bars *(100% cacao)*

Natural almond butter

Natural peanut butter *(organic)*

Nuts

Olives

Oven-baked cheese bites

Persian cucumbers

Pork belly

Psyllium husks

Riced cauliflower *(fresh and frozen)*

Spaghetti squash

Sparkling water

Spice blends: 21 Seasoning Salute, Everyday Seasoning, Everything but the Bagel Seasoning, Garlic Salt, Mushroom & Company Multipurpose Umami Seasoning Blend, Seasoning Salt

Spicy taco sauce

Sunflower seed butter

Toasted sesame oil

Unsweetened cocoa powder

Unsweetened coconut flakes

## Walmart

Almond milk

Avocado oil

Bacon

Butter *(grass-fed)*

Cheese crisps

Coconut flour

Coconut milk

Coconut oil

Cream cheese

Dark chocolate *(85% cacao or higher)*

Eggs

Ghee

Heavy cream

Keto sweeteners

Lily's sugar-free chocolate chips

MCT oil

Nuts and seeds

Pork rinds

Ratio Dairy Snacks *(a yogurt alternative)*

Rebel ice cream

Riced cauliflower *(fresh and frozen)*

Rotisserie chicken

Two Good Greek yogurt

Whisps cheese crisps

Xanthan gum

## Amazon

*Items that you can't find in your local grocery store can usually be ordered from Amazon.com.*

Almond flour

ChocZero chocolate chips

Coconut flour

Flavor extracts and flavorings *(such as banana extract and cornbread flavoring)*

Good Dee's baking mixes

HighKey products—cookies, snacks, cereal, and more

Keto sweeteners

Pork panko *(fine pork rind crumbs; use whenever finely crushed pork rinds are called for in the recipes in this book)*

Unflavored and unsweetened whey protein powder *(aka whey protein isolate)*

Xanthan gum

# My Favorite Kitchen Equipment

I'm a huge fan of kitchen gadgets and appliances. I probably have more than I need! But for this section, I've narrowed it down to my favorites. Whether you are a seasoned cook with a fully stocked kitchen or a new cook starting your collection, you'll probably find a few things here to add to your list.

## Cookware

### Cast-Iron Skillet

Every kitchen needs at least one 10-inch and one 12-inch cast-iron skillet. Cast-iron cookware is tough, maintains heat, and improves with age as it becomes seasoned. These days, most cast-iron skillets come preseasoned. When well cared for, a cast-iron skillet will last for generations.

### Dutch Oven

A Dutch oven is an all-purpose piece of cookware. I use mine for soups, stews, and deep-frying. A 6-quart Dutch oven is the most versatile size, and the one needed for the recipes in this book. But you'll probably want to own more than one because they come in such a wide range of colors and sizes. I like enameled Dutch ovens because they're easier to clean. There are several brands to fit all budgets: Lodge makes a lower-priced option, while Staub and Le Creuset are popular higher-end brands.

## Cooking Appliances

### Air Fryer

Air fryers are all the rage these days. I was hesitant to add yet another small appliance to my kitchen; I questioned whether I would really use it. Finally, I caved and bought one, and I'm so glad I did because it has truly become one of my most-used appliances. You can cook just about anything in an air fryer. I use it mostly to make bacon and burgers and to reheat leftovers (it makes leftovers taste like freshly made food!). An air fryer is not required for any of the recipes in this book, but I recommend adding one to your cooking arsenal.

### Instant Pot

Enter the modern-day pressure cooker. It's not a necessity, but it's really nice to have. Most of your favorite recipes can be made in an Instant Pot with a few simple adjustments. I frequently use mine to make hard-boiled eggs. The shells slide off effortlessly. There's also a slow cooker function if you don't have space for both an Instant Pot and a slow cooker (see below). Like the air fryer, you won't need an Instant Pot to make any of the recipes in this book, but I recommend owning one for general cooking.

### Slow Cooker

Slow cookers have long been a favorite appliance for busy families. They are inexpensive and help tenderize less expensive cuts of meat. They also use less electricity than an oven. A good size to own is 6 quarts.

## Other Appliances

### Blender

A blender is a must for milkshakes and smoothies. Either a handheld immersion blender or a countertop model works well depending on the job. An immersion blender can blend soups directly in the pot and is easy to clean, whereas a countertop blender is better for larger jobs, such as making drinks for more than one person. A high-powdered model is great for making homemade nut butters or pureeing extra thick sauces and mixtures to perfection.

### Food Processor

This appliance is great for the person who cooks a lot. It makes chopping, shredding, and slicing easier. You can also use it for purees and sauces. An 8-cup food processor is the size I recommend.

### Hand Mixer

A handheld electric mixer is much less expensive than a stand mixer and great for smaller jobs. It's easy to clean because you can put the attachments in the dishwasher.

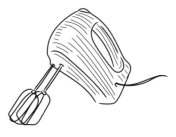

### Stand Mixer

A quality stand mixer is a workhorse. I've had the same one for almost fifteen years. It was a large investment but has paid off over time. It makes bigger jobs easier, freeing up my hands to do something else while the mixer takes care of the mixing. I sometimes use the dough hook attachment for meatloaf, making the job less messy.

Any recipe in this book that calls for a hand mixer can be made using a stand mixer instead.

## Bakeware

### Baking Sheets (aka Cookie Sheets)

Flat baking sheets are great for cookies, biscuits, and scones. I recommend having at least two. My baking sheets measure 18 by 12 inches—a standard size.

### Bundt Pan

I love my Bundt pans. They come in so many shapes and sizes. A 12-cup Bundt pan is the most common, and the size I use for my Zucchini Carrot Cake (page 214).

### Muffin Pan

A standard-size 12-cup muffin pan is essential, and not just for muffins. Muffin pans have so many creative uses: you can make mini quiches, meatloaves, and pies. A 24-cup mini muffin pan is a fun size to have as well but is not required for any of the recipes in this book.

### Parchment Paper

Parchment paper is one of my favorite kitchen items. Nothing sticks to it, and it makes cleanup a breeze! Don't confuse it with wax paper. If you don't have parchment paper on hand, in most cases you can use foil or grease the pan instead. Silicone baking mats are also a good option.

### Sheet Pans (aka Rimmed Baking Sheets)

Many recipes in this book use sheet pans. I have a number of them, some purchased at thrift stores (I love the look of a well-aged sheet pan). I use a standard-size sheet pan, 18 by 13 inches. I recommend owning at least two.

### Silicone Baking Cups

You can use these cups in place of a muffin pan or use them to line your muffin pan. They are more cost-effective than paper liners because they're reusable. The best part is that they are nonstick.

## Tools

### Candy Thermometer

A candy thermometer is an inexpensive tool that I mostly use to verify the temperature of oil when deep-frying. Keeping your oil at the proper temperature will ensure that your fried foods come out crispy rather than greasy.

### Kitchen Shears

Every kitchen needs a good pair of shears. You can use them to open food packages, break down poultry, cut bacon, and snip herbs.

### Knives

Buy the best knives you can afford. Moderately priced knives will last as long as more expensive ones if you care for them properly. Keep them sharpened and never put them in the dishwasher, where they can become dull.

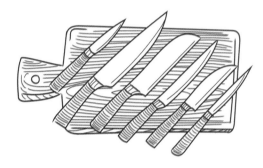

### Mesh Skimmer (aka Spider Strainer)

This inexpensive tool makes it easier and safer to remove foods from hot oil when deep-frying.

### Spiralizer

This gadget is handy for making zucchini noodles and other vegetable noodles. A handheld model can cost as little as $10. There are more expensive countertop models that are helpful for making large amounts of noodles.

## A Couple of Fun Extras

### Automatic Milk Frother

This is for you coffee lovers. It froths milk like a pro, elevating your average at-home drip coffees and lattes to coffeehouse levels! I use this tool to froth almond milk, coconut milk, and heavy cream. My favorite frother is the Nespresso Aeroccino.

Heavy cream has a high fat content and doesn't froth as readily as milk. Here's a hack for that: add a small amount of water to the cream, and it will froth amazingly well!

### Mini Waffle Maker

These little gadgets are everywhere these days, and for good reason. They cost about $10, and you can use them to make mini waffles that can serve as a bread replacement for sandwiches. One of the newest keto waffle crazes is chaffles, a portmanteau of *cheese* and *waffle.* A basic chaffle recipe is a combination of one large egg, whisked well, and ¼ cup of shredded mild, semisoft cheese, such as mozzarella or cheddar. This makes two mini chaffles that measure about 4 inches across—perfect for a sandwich. If you're new to chaffles, I would start with this basic recipe and then play around with different herbs, spices, and add-ins to create the flavors that you like. You can find many chaffle recipes and inspirations online.

# Lunch Box Ideas

Tired of eating the same thing over and over, people often asked me for lunch ideas. Well, these lunches—I call them "snack-y lunches"—are my favorite! They are great for adults and kids; they are also perfect for work and school. Even if you are at home all day, portioning lunches in advance saves you time. You can use a bento box as shown or any divided containers you choose. I purchased my bento boxes on Amazon.com. The stainless-steel options are more durable than plastic and easier to clean.

Ham or turkey

Babybel cheese

Dill pickles

Almonds

Hard-boiled egg with everything bagel seasoning

Deviled Ham (page 84)

Cheddar cheese

Cucumber slices

Pecans

Blackberries

Ham, cheese & pickle roll-ups

Cherry tomatoes

Walnuts

Raspberries

Sugar-free white chocolate chips

Tuna-stuffed mini sweet peppers

Cheese

Almonds

Parmesan crisps

Chocolate-covered strawberries

Chicken salad

Cheese

Celery sticks

Macadamia nuts

Blueberries

Pimento cheese

Everything Crackers (page 92)

Sliced mini sweet peppers

Raspberries

Pistachios

Salami, cream cheese & pickle roll-ups

Blackberries

Pork rinds

Spicy Sweet Almonds (page 78)

# Keto Charcuterie

Charcuterie boards are trendy, and rightfully so. They are beautiful and customizable and can easily feed a crowd. You can make your boards as simple or as elaborate as you please. Use your imagination and have fun with it!

I like to use a large wood serving board, but if you don't have one, use any serving tray you have on hand. You can even assemble the ingredients directly on your counter or buffet table: lay down a large sheet of parchment paper, then lay your meats and cheeses on top. Nuts, olives, and the like can go in small bowls.

A keto charcuterie board isn't much different from the typical one; you simply replace grain-based crackers and sugary jams with keto-friendly options. Choose from these examples:

## Deli Meats

Ham

Pepperoni

Prosciutto

Roast beef

Salami *(Calabrese, Genoa, peppered, etc.)*

Turkey

## Cheeses

Blue cheese

Brie

Cheddar

Feta

Goat cheese

Gruyère

Provolone

Smoked Gouda

## Nuts & Seeds

Almonds *(plain or Marcona)*

Macadamia nuts

Pecans

Pistachios

Pumpkin seeds, shelled

Sunflower seeds, shelled

Walnuts

## Berries

Blackberries

Blueberries

Raspberries

Strawberries

## Veggies

Banana peppers

Bell pepper slices

Celery sticks

Cucumber slices

Mini sweet peppers

Radish slices

## Miscellaneous

Baked Raspberry Walnut Brie (page 90)

Cheese balls or crisps

Chocolate *(dark or sugar-free)*

Everything Crackers (page 92)

Herb sprigs, such as rosemary and parsley, for garnish

Olives *(black and/or green)*

Pork rinds

Spicy Sweet Almonds (page 78)

Sugar-Free Raspberry Jam (page 274)

Sweet & Salty Snack Mix (page 102)

# What's for Dinner?
# Four Weeks of Sample Menus

It's the age-old question: what's for dinner? It's on your mind all day, and it's what the whole family wants to know. I've put together some sample dinner menus to make things easier for you. I've left Saturday as a free day for eating out or using up leftovers from the week, if you choose. Also, any leftovers from these meals make great lunches the next day.

## Week 1 Menu

### Sunday

**Shepherd's Pie
(page 142)**

### Monday

**Slow Cooker
Chicken Tacos
(page 174)**

### Tuesday

**Zuppa Toscana
(page 116) with
side salad**

### Wednesday

**Shrimp & Andouille
Sausage Jambalaya
(page 178)**

### Thursday

**Bacon Cheeseburger
Cauli-Rice Skillet
(page 150)**

### Friday

**Zucchini Parmesan
(page 138) with
Caesar salad**

## Saturday: No cooking!

# Week 1 Shopping List

## Meats

Andouille or other smoked sausage, 14 ounces

Bacon, 1 (8-ounce) package

Bulk Italian sausage, 1 pound

Chicken thighs (boneless and skinless), 2 pounds

Ground beef, 3 pounds

Medium shrimp, peeled and deveined, 1 pound

## Eggs & Dairy

Butter (salted), 8 ounces

Grated Parmesan cheese, 1 cup

Heavy cream, 1 pint

Large eggs, 3

Shredded cheddar cheese, 1½ cups

Shredded mozzarella cheese, 1 cup

## Produce

Celery, 1 bunch

Frozen cauliflower florets, 2 (16-ounce) bags

Frozen leaf spinach, 1 (10-ounce) package

Frozen riced cauliflower, 3 (10-ounce) bags

Garlic, 1 head

Green bell pepper, 1 medium

Mushrooms, sliced, 1 (8-ounce) package

Romaine lettuce, 1 head

Side salad ingredients of your choice

Yellow onions, 2 medium

Zucchini, 2 medium

## Pantry Items

Avocado oil, 2 tablespoons

Beef broth, 1 (14-ounce) can

Diced green chilies, 1 (4-ounce) can

Dill pickle, 1 large

Dill pickle relish, 1 tablespoon

Liquid stevia

Marinara sauce, 1 cup

Mayonnaise, ½ cup

Petite diced tomatoes, 2 (14.5-ounce) cans

Pork rind crumbs, 1 (12-ounce) jar

Prepared yellow mustard, 2 tablespoons

Taco shells (keto-friendly), 10

Tomato sauce, 1 (8-ounce) can

Vegetable broth, 1 (32-ounce) carton

Worcestershire sauce, 3 tablespoons

## Dried Herbs & Spices

Bay leaf, 1

Cayenne pepper, ¼ teaspoon

Chili powder, 2 tablespoons

Dried dill weed, 1 teaspoon

Dried minced onions, 1 tablespoon

Dried oregano leaves, ½ teaspoon

Dried thyme leaves, ¼ teaspoon

Garlic powder, ½ teaspoon

Ground black pepper, 1½ teaspoons

Ground cumin, 1 tablespoon

Ground dried oregano, ½ teaspoon

Italian seasoning, 4 teaspoons

Paprika, 2 teaspoons

Seasoning salt, 1 teaspoon

# Week 2 Menu

### Sunday

Slow Cooker
Cheesesteak
Pot Roast
(page 186)

### Monday

Sheet Pan Smoked
Sausage & Cabbage
(page 132)

### Tuesday

Blackened Salmon
(page 180) with
Asiago Roasted
Green Beans
(page 200)

### Wednesday

Lasagna-Stuffed
Spaghetti Squash
(page 166)

### Thursday

Green Chile
Chicken Soup
(page 122) with
side salad

### Friday

Roast Beef &
Caramelized Onion
Pizza (page 160)

Saturday: No cooking!

# Week 2 Shopping List

## Meats

Beef chuck roast, 3 to 4 pounds

Chicken thighs (boneless and skinless), 1 pound

Deli roast beef, 8 ounces

Ground beef, 1 pound

Salmon fillets, 3 pounds

Smoked rope sausage, 12 ounces

## Eggs & Dairy

Butter (salted), 8 ounces

Cream cheese, 2 ounces

Grated Parmesan cheese, 1 cup

Heavy cream, 1 pint

Large egg, 1

Ricotta cheese, 1 cup

Shredded Asiago cheese, 1 cup

Shredded cheddar cheese, 1 cup

Shredded mozzarella cheese, 4 cups

Sour cream, 1 (8-ounce) tub

## Produce

Garlic, 1 bulb

Green beans, 1 pound

Green bell pepper, 1 medium

Green cabbage, ½ head

Jalapeño pepper, 1

Red bell peppers, 2 medium

Red cabbage, ½ head

Sliced mushrooms, 1 (8-ounce) package

Spaghetti squash, 1 (3-pound)

Yellow onions, 3 medium

## Pantry Items

Avocado oil, ¾ cup

Baking powder, 2 teaspoons

Beef broth, 1 (14-ounce) can

Blanched almond flour, ¾ cup

Brown sugar substitute, 1 tablespoon

Chicken broth, 1 (32-ounce) carton

Diced green chilies, 1 (4-ounce) can

Marinara sauce, 1 (16-ounce) jar

Salt, 2 tablespoons

Worcestershire sauce, 2 tablespoons

## Dried Herbs & Spices

Cayenne pepper, 2 teaspoons

Dried basil, 2 teaspoons

Dried parsley, 1 teaspoon

Dried thyme leaves, ½ teaspoon

Garlic powder, 1 teaspoon

Ground black pepper, 1 tablespoon

Ground cumin, 2 teaspoons

Ground dried oregano, 2 teaspoons

Ground mustard, ½ teaspoon

Onion powder, 1 teaspoon

Smoked paprika, 2 tablespoons

# Week 3 Menu

### Sunday

Country Fried Steak &
Gravy (page 134) with
Roasted Garlic Chive
Cauli-Mash (page 210)

### Monday

Garlic Parmesan
Shrimp (page 136)

### Tuesday

Cheesy Green Chile
Pork Chops
(page 164)

### Wednesday

Ground Beef
Teriyaki Bowl
(page 144)

### Thursday

Meatball Marinara
(page 140)

### Friday

Nashville Hot
Chicken Tenders
(page 170)

## Saturday: No cooking!

# Week 3 Shopping List

## Meats

Bulk breakfast sausage, 1 pound

Chicken tenderloins, 2 pounds

Cube steaks, 4 (4 ounces each)

Ground beef, 2 pounds

Medium shrimp, peeled and deveined, 1 pound

Pork chops, bone-in or boneless, 4 (1 inch thick)

## Eggs & Dairy

Butter (salted), 8 ounces

Cream cheese, 4 ounces

Grated Parmesan cheese, 1 cup

Heavy cream, 1 pint

Large eggs, 3

Provolone cheese, 6 slices

Shredded Monterey Jack cheese, 1 cup

Shredded mozzarella cheese, 1 cup

Shredded Parmesan cheese, ½ cup

Sour cream, 2 tablespoons

## Produce

Basil, 1 bunch

Chives, 1 (0.5-ounce) package

Frozen cauliflower florets, 2 (12-ounce) bags

Garlic, 2 heads

## Pantry Items

Avocado oil, 2 tablespoons

Brown sugar substitute, ½ cup

Coconut aminos, ¼ cup

Diced green chilies, 1 (4-ounce) can

Dill pickle chips. ½ cup

Extra-virgin olive oil, 3 tablespoons

Kosher salt

Maple syrup (sugar-free), 2 tablespoons

Marinara sauce, 1 (16-ounce) jar

Oil, for deep-frying

Pork rind crumbs, ¾ cup

Salt, 2 tablespoons

Toasted sesame oil, 1 tablespoon

Unseasoned rice vinegar, 1 tablespoon

Whey protein powder (unflavored and unsweetened), 1 cup

Xanthan gum, ¼ teaspoon

## Dried Herbs & Spices

Cayenne pepper, 2 tablespoons

Chili powder, ½ teaspoon

Dried basil, ½ teaspoon

Dried parsley, 2 teaspoons

Garlic powder, 1 tablespoon

Ginger powder, 2 tablespoons

Ground black pepper, 2 tablespoons

Ground cumin, ½ teaspoon

Ground dried oregano, 1 teaspoon

Onion powder, ½ teaspoon

Paprika, 3 teaspoons

Red pepper flakes

Smoked paprika, ½ teaspoon

# Week 4 Menu

### Sunday

Brown Sugar–Glazed
Meatloaf (page 154) with
Sheet Pan Parmesan
Yellow Squash & Zucchini
(page 208)

### Monday

Easy Buffalo
Chicken Soup
(page 124) with
side salad

### Tuesday

Fiesta Casserole
(page 176)

### Wednesday

Shrimp Alfredo
Spaghetti Squash
(page 146)

### Thursday

Pork Fried Rice
(page 152)

### Friday

Corn Dog Casserole
(page 158)

## Saturday: No cooking!

# Week 4 Shopping List

## Meats

Beef hot dogs, 4

Bulk breakfast sausage, 1 pound

Ground beef, 3½ pounds

Medium shrimp, peeled and deveined, 1 pound

Rotisserie chicken, 1

## Eggs & Dairy

Butter (salted), 2 tablespoons

Cream cheese, 12 ounces

Grated Parmesan cheese, 1 cup

Heavy cream, 1 pint

Large eggs, 5

Shredded cheddar cheese, ½ cup

Shredded Mexican blend cheese, ½ cup

Shredded Parmesan cheese, 1½ cups

## Produce

Celery, 1 bunch

Frozen riced cauliflower, 3 (12-ounce) bags

Garlic, 2 heads

Green onions, 1 bunch

Parsley, 1 bunch

Red bell pepper, 1

Side salad ingredients of your choice

Spaghetti squash, 1 (3 pounds)

Yellow squash, 2 medium

Zucchini, 2 medium

## Pantry Items

Avocado oil, ¼ cup

Baking powder, 1 teaspoon

Beef broth, ½ cup

Blanched almond flour, ¾ cup

Brown sugar substitute, ½ cup

Buffalo sauce, ¼ cup *(see page 273 for ingredients)*

Chicken broth, 1 (24-ounce) carton

Diced tomatoes and green chilies, 1 (10-ounce) can

Ketchup (no sugar added), ¾ cup

Pure sweet corn extract, ½ teaspoon

Salt, 1 tablespoon

Toasted sesame oil, 2 tablespoons

Tomato paste, 1 (12-ounce) can

Worcestershire sauce, 2 tablespoons

## Dried Herbs & Spices

Chili powder, 2 tablespoons

Dried chives, 1 teaspoon

Dried minced onions, 1 tablespoon

Dried parsley, 2 teaspoons

Ginger powder, 3 teaspoons

Ground black pepper, 1 teaspoon

Ground cumin, 1 tablespoon

Paprika, 1 teaspoon

Red pepper flakes, ½ teaspoon

# Themed Menu Ideas

Need some ideas for putting meals together, whether you're cooking for date night or looking for an easy but satisfying combination of recipes? Here are some suggestions for various themes. Feel free to make your own substitutions!

## Breakfast for Dinner

Breakfast Pizza Casserole (page 48)

Strawberry Breakfast Cake (page 58)

Bacon

Berries

## Italian Night

Antipasto Salad with Creamy Italian Dressing (page 114)

Meatball Marinara (page 140)

Zucchini noodles

Lemon Cheesecake Mousse (page 218)

## Game Night

Easy Buffalo Chicken Soup (page 124)

Jalapeño Popper Dip (page 74)

Roast Beef & Caramelized Onion Pizza (page 160)

Lisa's Peanut Butter Cheesecake Brownies (page 236)

## Kid-Friendly Feast

Corn Dog Casserole (page 158)

Roasted Cheesy Cauli-Mac (page 194)

Muddy Buddies (page 228)

## Taco Tuesday

Slow Cooker Chicken Tacos
(page 174)

Cilantro Lime Cauli-Rice (page 202)

Frozen Strawberry Margaritas
(page 262)

## Soup and Salad Night

Spinach Strawberry Salad (page 108)

Green Chicken Chile Soup
(page 122)

Savory Skillet Zucchini Bread
(page 70)

Loaded N'oatmeal Cookies
(page 220)

## Date Night

Blackened Salmon (page 180)

Lump Crab Cakes with Chipotle
Mayo (page 148)

Mushroom Cauli-Risotto (page 196)

Skillet Blondie for Two (page 232)

## Southern Comfort Food

Country Fried Steak & Gravy
(page 134)

Roasted Garlic Chive Cauli-Mash
(page 210)

Southern Summer Squash Casserole
(page 206)

Red Velvet Cake (page 250)

# ❋ Recipes ❋

This section is filled with easy-to-make recipes that are family friendly. My own family enjoyed trying them all, and many of these recipes have become staples in our home. I hope you enjoy them as much as we do!

I've marked recipes that are free of common allergens with icons:

 Nut-free (I've included peanuts in this category, even though peanuts are technically legumes.)

 Dairy-free

 Egg-free

 Ready in 30 minutes or less

For a handy chart showing which recipes fall into each of these categories, see pages 284 to 286.

Nutrition information is included for each recipe as well. It was calculated to the best of my ability, using information from my preferred brands of ingredients. Optional or suggested ingredients are not included in these calculations. Neither is oil used for frying foods; the amount of oil absorbed simply cannot be calculated accurately. I always recommend calculating your own macros; they can vary widely depending on the brands of ingredients you use. There are apps you can use for this task, such as KetoDietApp.

## Chapter 2
# ❧ Breakfast & Breads ❧

# Maple Brown Sugar N'oatmeal

yield: 1 serving • prep time: 10 minutes • cook time: 10 minutes

½ cup unsweetened almond milk

2 tablespoons brown sugar substitute

1 tablespoon chia seeds

1 tablespoon hemp hearts

1 tablespoon sugar-free maple syrup

¼ teaspoon pure vanilla extract

Pinch of salt

Nuts of choice, for garnish (optional)

Unsweetened coconut flakes, for garnish (optional)

1. Place all of the ingredients in a small saucepan over medium heat. Cook, stirring occasionally, for 10 minutes, until the mixture starts to bubble and thicken.

2. Remove the pan from the heat and allow to sit for 5 minutes. The n'oatmeal will thicken up as it sits. Garnish with nuts and coconut flakes, if desired.

NET CARBS 2.2g

| calories | fat | protein | carbs | fiber |
|----------|-----|---------|-------|-------|
| 156 | 9.7g | 5.7g | 6g | 3.9g |

# Breakfast Pizza Casserole

yield: 8 servings • prep time: 5 minutes • cook time: 45 minutes

1 pound bulk breakfast sausage

½ teaspoon garlic powder

½ teaspoon dried minced onions

½ teaspoon ground dried oregano

¼ teaspoon dried basil

10 large eggs

¼ cup heavy cream

½ teaspoon ground black pepper

½ cup shredded mozzarella cheese

½ cup pepperoni slices

½ cup sliced mushrooms

¼ cup sliced black olives

1. Preheat the oven to 375°F. Grease a 9 by 13-inch baking dish with oil.

2. In a medium-size skillet over medium heat, cook the sausage with the garlic powder, dried minced onions, oregano, and basil, crumbling the meat as it cooks, until the sausage is well browned and cooked through, about 10 minutes. Drain any excess fat and set aside.

3. Whisk the eggs, cream, and pepper in a medium-size bowl until well combined. Stir in the cooked sausage and cheese. Pour into the prepared casserole dish. Top with the pepperoni, mushrooms, and olives.

4. Bake for 30 to 35 minutes, until the center is set and the edges are lightly browned. Serve immediately. Leftovers can be stored in an airtight container in the refrigerator for up to a week. Reheat just until warmed; be careful not to overheat or the eggs will become rubbery.

*Note: I love leftover pizza for breakfast, and I love breakfast casseroles. This recipe combines the best of both worlds! You can customize the toppings to your liking.*

NET CARBS 1.8g

| calories | fat | protein | carbs | fiber |
|---|---|---|---|---|
| 361 | 27.8g | 20.6g | 2.9g | 1.2g |

# Cinnamon Pull-Apart Bread

yield: 6 servings • prep time: 15 minutes • cook time: 25 minutes

**2 cups finely shredded mozzarella cheese**

**2 ounces cream cheese (¼ cup)**

**½ cup finely ground blanched almond flour**

**¼ cup plus 2 teaspoons granular sweetener, divided**

**1 tablespoon coconut flour**

**2 teaspoons baking powder**

**2 teaspoons ground cinnamon, divided**

**1 large egg, whisked**

**Glaze:**

**1 ounce cream cheese (2 tablespoons), softened**

**1 tablespoon confectioners' sweetener**

**2 tablespoons heavy cream**

1. Preheat the oven to 375°F. Line an 8 by 4-inch loaf pan with parchment paper.

2. Put the mozzarella and cream cheese in a medium-size microwave-safe bowl. Microwave until melted, stirring every 30 seconds.

3. Add the almond flour, ¼ cup of the granular sweetener, the coconut flour, the baking powder, 1 teaspoon of the cinnamon, and the egg and stir with a rubber spatula until the ingredients are well combined and a firm dough comes together. Place the dough in the refrigerator for 10 minutes.

4. In a small bowl, stir together the remaining 2 teaspoons of granular sweetener and 1 teaspoon of cinnamon. Tear off small pieces of the dough and roll them into balls about 1 inch in diameter. Roll each ball in the cinnamon mixture. Place the dough balls in the prepared pan, side by side. Bake for 20 to 25 minutes, or until golden brown.

5. While the bread is baking, make the glaze: Stir together the cream cheese, confectioners' sweetener, and cream in a small bowl. Pour the glaze over the warm bread. Let sit for 15 minutes before serving. Leftovers can be stored in an airtight container in the refrigerator for up to a week.

*Note: Not having to roll out and cut out the dough makes this recipe for cinnamon rolls a bit simpler. You get the same delicious flavors with less work!*

NET CARBS 2.5g

| calories | fat | protein | carbs | fiber |
|----------|-----|---------|-------|-------|
| 260 | 20.4g | 13.7g | 5g | 2.6g |

# Breakfast Sandwich "Buns"

yield: 1 serving · prep time: 5 minutes · cook time: 5 minutes

1 large egg

1 tablespoon coconut flour

1 tablespoon heavy cream

1 tablespoon sugar-free maple syrup

1 teaspoon granular sweetener

½ teaspoon baking powder

¼ teaspoon pure vanilla extract

1. In a small bowl, mix together all of the ingredients.

2. Lightly grease a medium-size skillet and set it over medium heat. Pour half of the batter into one side of the skillet to make a small pancake, then pour in the remainder of the batter to make a second small pancake. Cook until browned on both sides, about 2½ minutes per side.

*Notes: These pancakes can also be made using a Dash Mini Maker Griddle. It makes the perfect size!*

*Use the pancakes to make a breakfast sandwich with your desired filling ingredients. My favorites are a fried egg and bacon or sausage (and sometimes both!).*

NET CARBS 1.7g

| calories | fat | protein | carbs | fiber |
|----------|-----|---------|-------|-------|
| 187 | 11.8g | 7.8g | 3g | 1.3g |

# Blueberry Lemon Coffee Cake

yield: 8 servings · prep time: 10 minutes · cook time: 30 minutes

1½ cups finely ground blanched almond flour

¼ cup coconut flour

2 teaspoons baking powder

¼ teaspoon salt

½ cup (1 stick) salted butter, softened

½ cup granular sweetener

3 large eggs

1 teaspoon pure vanilla extract

Grated zest and juice of 1 lemon

¾ cup blueberries

Crumble:

¼ cup (½ stick) cold salted butter, cubed

¼ cup finely ground blanched almond flour

¼ cup granular sweetener

½ teaspoon ground cinnamon

1. Preheat the oven to 350°F. Grease a 9-inch round cake pan with oil.

2. In a medium-size bowl, whisk together the flours, baking powder, and salt.

3. In a stand mixer fitted with the whisk attachment, or in a large mixing bowl using a hand mixer, cream the butter and sweetener on medium speed until fluffy, 1 to 2 minutes. Beat in the eggs one at a time. Blend in the vanilla, lemon zest, and juice.

4. With the mixer on low speed, add the flour mixture ½ cup at a time. After all of the flour mixture has been incorporated, use a spoon to gently stir in the blueberries. Spoon the batter into the prepared pan, then smooth the top.

5. To make the crumble, use a fork to mix the ingredients together in a small bowl until pea-size crumbles form. Sprinkle the crumble evenly over the batter.

6. Bake for 30 minutes, or until a toothpick or tester inserted in the middle of the cake comes out clean. Place the pan on a wire rack and allow the cake to cool completely.

7. To serve, gently loosen the sides of the cooled cake from the pan with a knife and transfer it to a cake plate, if desired. Leftovers can be stored in an airtight container in the refrigerator for up to a week.

NET CARBS 5.6g

| calories | fat | protein | carbs | fiber |
|---|---|---|---|---|
| 389 | 36.2g | 9.9g | 9.9g | 4.3g |

# Grain-Free Granola Bars

yield: 10 bars (1 per serving) · prep time: 10 minutes, plus 2 hours to chill

½ cup sliced almonds

½ cup roasted and salted shelled sunflower seeds

½ cup unsweetened shredded coconut

½ cup natural almond butter

¼ cup coconut oil, melted

¼ cup sugar-free maple syrup

2 tablespoons granular sweetener

1. Line a 9-inch square baking dish with parchment paper.

2. In a medium-size bowl, mix together all of the ingredients. Press the mixture into the prepared baking dish. Refrigerate for at least 2 hours.

3. Use a sharp knife to cut into bars. Leftovers can be stored in an airtight container for up to 2 weeks.

NET CARBS 2.9g

| calories | fat | protein | carbs | fiber |
|---|---|---|---|---|
| 239 | 19.3g | 6.1g | 12.2g | 9.3g |

# Strawberry Breakfast Cake

yield: 6 servings · prep time: 10 minutes · cook time: 30 minutes

1½ cups finely ground blanched almond flour

½ cup granular sweetener

2 teaspoons baking powder

¼ teaspoon salt

2 large eggs

¼ cup heavy cream

½ teaspoon pure vanilla extract

½ cup sliced strawberries, plus whole berries for garnish if desired

Glaze (Optional):

¼ cup heavy cream

¼ cup confectioners' sweetener

1. Preheat the oven to 350°F. Grease a 9-inch round cake pan.

2. In a small bowl, whisk together the almond flour, granular sweetener, baking powder, and salt.

3. In a medium-size mixing bowl, whisk the eggs, then stir in the cream and vanilla. Slowly add the flour mixture, stirring until well blended. Gently stir in the strawberries.

4. Pour the batter into the prepared pan and smooth the top.

5. Bake for 25 to 30 minutes, or until a toothpick or tester inserted in the middle of the cake comes out clean.

6. While the cake is baking, make the glaze, if using: Mix the cream and confectioners' sweetener in a small bowl until the sweetener is fully dissolved and the glaze is smooth; set aside.

7. Allow the cake to cool completely in the pan, then gently loosen the sides with a knife and transfer the cake to a cake plate. Pour the glaze evenly over the top, if using, before cutting and serving. Leftovers can be stored in an airtight container in the refrigerator for up to a week.

WITHOUT GLAZE NET CARBS 3.3g

| calories | fat | protein | carbs | fiber |
|---|---|---|---|---|
| 186 | 15.7g | 7.5g | 6.1g | 2.8g |

# Low-Carb Banana Bread

yield: one 8 by 4-inch loaf (8 servings) · prep time: 15 minutes
cook time: 40 minutes

1½ cups finely ground blanched almond flour

½ cup brown sugar substitute

2 teaspoons baking powder

½ teaspoon ground cinnamon

½ teaspoon xanthan gum

¼ teaspoon salt

2 large eggs

2 tablespoons heavy cream

2 tablespoons salted butter, melted

2 teaspoons pure banana extract

1. Preheat the oven to 350°F. Grease an 8 by 4-inch loaf pan or line it with parchment paper.

2. In a small bowl, whisk together the almond flour, brown sugar substitute, baking powder, cinnamon, xanthan gum, and salt.

3. In a large bowl, whisk the eggs until frothy, then add the cream, melted butter, and banana extract. Whisk until blended. Slowly stir in the flour mixture with a spoon until the batter is well combined.

4. Spread the batter evenly in the prepared loaf pan. Bake for 35 to 40 minutes, or until a toothpick or tester inserted in the middle of the loaf comes out clean.

5. Allow to completely cool before removing from the pan and slicing. Leftovers can be stored in an airtight container at room temperature for up to 3 days or in the refrigerator for up to a week.

*Note: My banana bread-loving husband couldn't believe that this bread doesn't have actual bananas in it. The secret to keeping it low-carb is using banana extract. For the best taste, make sure to use real banana extract, not imitation flavoring.*

NET CARBS 2.2g

| calories | fat | protein | carbs | fiber |
|----------|-------|---------|-------|-------|
| 169 | 15.2g | 5.7g | 4g | 2.4g |

# Jalapeño Cheddar Scones

yield: 8 scones (1 per serving) · prep time: 15 minutes, plus 30 minutes to chill
cook time: 20 minutes

½ cup plus 2 tablespoons heavy cream, divided

1 teaspoon white vinegar

3 cups finely ground blanched almond flour

1 cup shredded sharp cheddar cheese

1 tablespoon baking powder

½ teaspoon salt

½ teaspoon xanthan gum

½ cup (1 stick) cold salted butter, cubed

1 large egg

2 tablespoons seeded and finely diced jalapeño peppers, plus 8 jalapeño slices for garnish

1. In a small bowl, combine ½ cup of the cream and the vinegar; set aside.

2. In a large bowl, whisk together the almond flour, cheese, baking powder, salt, and xanthan gum until combined. Add the butter to the bowl. Use a fork or pastry blender to cut the butter into the flour mixture until pea-size crumbles form.

3. Add the egg to the cream mixture and whisk to combine. Pour the cream mixture into the dry mixture and use a spoon to gently mix the two together just until combined. Add the diced jalapeños and stir to incorporate them, but don't overwork the dough.

4. Line a baking sheet with parchment paper and set aside. Turn the dough out onto another piece of parchment paper. Use your hands to gently shape the dough into a circle, about 2 inches thick. Use a sharp knife to cut the circle into 8 wedges. Transfer the scones to the prepared baking sheet, spacing them 2 to 3 inches apart. Gently press a jalapeño slice into the top of each scone. Place the baking sheet in the refrigerator to chill the dough for 30 minutes.

5. Preheat the oven to 400°F.

6. Brush the scones with the remaining 2 tablespoons of cream. Bake until golden brown, 15 to 20 minutes. Serve immediately. Leftovers can be stored in an airtight container in the refrigerator for up to a week.

NET CARBS 4.4g

| calories | fat | protein | carbs | fiber |
|---|---|---|---|---|
| 515 | 47.7g | 16.4g | 8.3g | 3.9g |

# Bacon Pimento Cheese Muffins

yield: 10 muffins (1 per serving) · prep time: 10 minutes · cook time: 18 minutes

**1 cup finely ground blanched almond flour**

**2 tablespoons coconut flour**

**2 teaspoons baking powder**

**½ teaspoon smoked paprika**

**¼ teaspoon garlic powder**

**¼ teaspoon onion powder**

**¼ teaspoon salt**

**¼ teaspoon ground black pepper**

**2 large eggs**

**½ cup mayonnaise**

**1 cup shredded sharp cheddar cheese**

**2 tablespoons pimentos, drained**

**4 slices bacon, partially cooked and diced**

1. Preheat the oven to 375°F. Grease 10 wells of a standard-size 12-cup muffin pan, or line them with parchment paper liners or silicone baking cups.

2. In a medium-size bowl, whisk together the flours, baking powder, paprika, garlic powder, onion powder, salt, and pepper.

3. In a small bowl, whisk the eggs, then stir in the mayonnaise. Pour the wet mixture into the flour mixture and stir until well combined. Gently fold the cheese and pimentos into the batter.

4. Spoon the batter into the prepared muffin wells, filling them about three-quarters full. Top the muffins with the bacon. Bake for 15 to 18 minutes, or until a toothpick or tester inserted in the middle of a muffin comes out clean.

5. Allow the muffins to cool completely before removing them from the pan. Leftovers can be stored in an airtight container in the refrigerator for up to a week.

NET CARBS 1.8g

| calories | fat | protein | carbs | fiber |
|---|---|---|---|---|
| 266 | 24.3g | 10.3g | 3g | 1.2g |

# Caramelized Onion & Bacon Frittata

yield: 6 servings · prep time: 10 minutes · cook time: 50 minutes

**2 tablespoons salted butter**

**1 medium onion, sliced**

**8 large eggs**

**¼ cup heavy cream**

**½ teaspoon ground black pepper**

**¼ teaspoon ground nutmeg**

**¼ teaspoon salt**

**6 slices bacon, cooked and crumbled**

**1 cup shredded Swiss cheese**

1. Preheat the oven to 375°F.

2. Melt the butter in a 12-inch cast-iron skillet or other ovenproof skillet over medium heat. Add the onion and sauté until caramelized, about 30 minutes, stirring every few minutes. Toward the end of cooking, stir them often; be careful not to burn them. They should be golden brown. Remove the pan from the heat.

3. In a medium-size mixing bowl, whisk together the eggs, cream, pepper, nutmeg, and salt. Pour the egg mixture evenly over the onion. Sprinkle with the bacon and cheese. Bake for 20 minutes, or until the eggs are set.

4. Run a knife around the edge of the skillet before slicing the frittata. Serve immediately. Leftovers can be stored in an airtight container in the refrigerator for up to 5 days.

NET CARBS 1.3g

| calories | fat | protein | carbs | fiber |
|---|---|---|---|---|
| 256 | 15.5g | 17g | 1.5g | 0.4g |

# "Apple" Pie Muffins

yield: 12 muffins (1 per serving) • prep time: 15 minutes • cook time: 30 minutes

1½ cups finely ground blanched almond flour

¼ cup granular sweetener

2 teaspoons apple pie spice

2 teaspoons baking powder

¼ teaspoon salt

1 medium zucchini

2 large eggs

¼ cup sour cream

½ teaspoon pure vanilla extract

**Crumble Topping:**

¼ cup finely ground blanched almond flour

2 tablespoons brown sugar substitute

¼ cup (½ stick) cold salted butter, cubed

1. Preheat the oven to 350°F. Grease a standard-size 12-cup muffin pan.

2. In a small bowl, whisk together the almond flour, granular sweetener, apple pie spice, baking powder, and salt.

3. Peel the zucchini, leaving behind no green skin. Cut it into quarters lengthwise and cut away the seeds. Finely dice the zucchini and use paper towels to remove any excess liquid.

4. In a medium-size bowl, whisk the eggs, then stir in the sour cream and vanilla. Slowly add the flour mixture, stirring until well blended. Gently stir in the zucchini.

5. Pour the batter into the prepared muffin pan, filling each well about three-quarters full.

6. To make the crumble topping, put the almond flour and brown sugar substitute in a small bowl and use a fork or pastry blender to stir them together. Add the butter and continue stirring until the mixture is crumbly.

7. Sprinkle the muffins evenly with crumble topping. Bake for 25 to 30 minutes, until the topping is lightly browned and a toothpick or tester inserted in the middle of a muffin comes out clean.

8. Allow the muffins to cool completely before removing them from the pan. Leftovers can be stored in an airtight container on the counter for up to 3 days or in the refrigerator for up to a week.

*Note: I know what you're thinking: apples aren't keto. The secret ingredient is zucchini. I love how this mild-tasting veggie takes on the flavor and texture of apples in these tender, delicious muffins.*

NET CARBS 2.7g

| calories | fat | protein | carbs | fiber |
|----------|-----|---------|-------|-------|
| 183 | 16.6g | 5.8g | 5.1g | 2.4g |

# Savory Skillet Zucchini Bread

yield: 8 servings • prep time: 15 minutes • cook time: 30 minutes

**2 tablespoons salted butter**

**2 cups finely ground blanched almond four**

**2 teaspoons baking powder**

**1 teaspoon baking soda**

**½ teaspoon garlic powder**

**½ teaspoon salt**

**½ teaspoon xanthan gum**

**2 large eggs**

**½ cup sour cream**

**1 cup shredded cheddar cheese**

**1 cup shredded zucchini**

1. Preheat the oven to 375°F.

2. Put the butter in a 10-inch cast-iron skillet or other ovenproof skillet and place the pan in the oven to melt the butter.

3. In a large bowl, whisk together the almond flour, baking powder, baking soda, garlic powder, salt, and xanthan gum.

4. In a small bowl, whisk together the eggs and sour cream. Stir the sour cream mixture into the almond flour mixture until well combined. Fold in the cheese and zucchini.

5. Pour the batter into the prepared skillet and bake for 25 to 30 minutes, until lightly browned on top and around the edges. Leftovers can be stored in an airtight container in the refrigerator for up to 5 days.

*Note: Here's a simple and delicious recipe for your abundant zucchini harvest. This savory bread is a nice break from more traditional sweet zucchini breads. It has a texture that's a bit like cornbread, and it's wonderful served with soup.*

NET CARBS 4g

| calories | fat | protein | carbs | fiber |
|----------|-----|---------|-------|-------|
| 281 | 24.8g | 10.7g | 6.7g | 2.8g |

*Chapter 3*

 # Appetizers & Snacks

# Jalapeño Popper Dip

yield: 6 servings • prep time: 15 minutes • cook time: 25 minutes

**2 (8-ounce) packages cream cheese, softened**

**½ cup sour cream**

**4 jalapeño peppers, seeded and chopped, plus sliced jalapeños for garnish**

**1 (4-ounce) can diced green chilies**

**1 clove garlic, minced**

**1 cup shredded cheddar cheese**

**8 slices bacon, cooked and crumbled**

Serving Suggestions:

**Pork rinds**

1. Preheat the oven to 375°F. Grease a 2-quart baking dish with oil.

2. In a medium-size bowl, stir together the cream cheese, sour cream, chopped jalapeños, chilies, and garlic until well combined. Fold in the cheddar and most of the bacon, reserving some bacon for garnish.

3. Spread the dip evenly in the prepared baking dish. Bake for 20 to 25 minutes, until the dip is bubbling around the edges and browned on top.

4. Garnish with the reserved bacon and the jalapeño slices. Serve with the dippers of your choice. Leftover dip can be stored in an airtight container in the refrigerator for up to 5 days.

*Notes: Jalapeno poppers are a favorite appetizer among low-carbers. Here, I took those ingredients and made them into a delicious dip. Crispy bacon makes a great dipper!*

*You can leave the seeds in the jalapeños if you like extra spicy foods.*

NET CARBS 2.7g

| calories | fat | protein | carbs | fiber |
|---|---|---|---|---|
| 437 | 40.7g | 14.3g | 3.4g | 0.8g |

# Dill Pickle Poppers

yield: 12 poppers (2 per serving) · prep time: 5 minutes · cook time: 25 minutes

**6 whole dill pickles**

**1 (8-ounce) package cream cheese, softened**

**12 thin-cut slices bacon**

**Freshly ground black pepper (optional)**

1. Preheat the oven to 425°F. Line a sheet pan with parchment paper.

2. Cut the pickles in half lengthwise and scoop out the seeds. Fill each pickle half with cream cheese, then wrap with a slice of bacon. Sprinkle with pepper, if desired.

3. Place the wrapped pickles in the prepared pan. Bake for 20 to 25 minutes, until the bacon reaches the desired crispness. Allow to rest for 10 minutes before serving. Best if eaten the same day.

*Note: These poppers are great served with ranch dressing; see page 268 for a recipe.*

NET CARBS 1.6g

| calories | fat | protein | carbs | fiber |
|----------|-----|---------|-------|-------|
| 228 | 16.8g | 9g | 1.6g | 0.1g |

# Spicy Sweet Almonds

yield: 2½ cups (¼ cup per serving) · prep time: 5 minutes · cook time: 25 minutes

**1 large egg white**

**2 tablespoons brown sugar substitute**

**1 teaspoon kosher-size salt**

**1 teaspoon smoked paprika**

**½ teaspoon cayenne pepper**

**2½ cups raw almonds**

1. Preheat the oven to 325°F. Line a sheet pan with parchment paper.

2. In a medium-size bowl, whisk the egg white until frothy, then stir in the brown sugar substitute, salt, paprika, and cayenne pepper. Fold in the almonds and stir until they are completely coated in the egg white mixture.

3. Spread the almonds evenly in the prepared pan. Bake for 25 minutes, stirring every 5 to 10 minutes, until nicely browned and aromatic. Allow to cool completely before serving. Leftovers can be stored in an airtight container for up to 2 weeks.

*Note: Flavored nuts are great for snacking, packing in lunch boxes, or serving on a charcuterie board. The grocery store varieties tend to contain a lot of unnecessary ingredients. This simple-to-make recipe is a good one to prepare ahead of time because the longer the almonds sit, the more the flavor develops.*

NET CARBS 3.4g

| calories | fat | protein | carbs | fiber |
|---|---|---|---|---|
| 210 | 17.9g | 8g | 8g | 4.6g |

# Shrimp Spread with Parmesan Crisps

yield: 6 servings · prep time: 10 minutes, plus 1 hour to chill

cook time: 10 minutes

½ cup ketchup (no sugar added)

½ cup mayonnaise

1 tablespoon prepared horseradish

1 teaspoon freshly squeezed lemon juice

1 teaspoon Worcestershire sauce

1 cup chopped cooked shrimp

1 (8-ounce) package cream cheese, softened

¼ cup sliced green onions

1 cup shredded Parmesan cheese, for the crisps

1. In a medium-size mixing bowl, stir together the ketchup, mayonnaise, horseradish, lemon juice, and Worcestershire until well combined. Fold in the shrimp.

2. Spread the cream cheese evenly on a serving plate. Top with the shrimp mixture and then the green onions. Place in the refrigerator to chill for 1 hour.

3. Meanwhile, make the Parmesan crisps: Line a microwave-safe plate with parchment paper. Spoon small piles of the Parmesan cheese onto the parchment, spacing them 2 inches apart. Microwave for 1 minute 30 seconds or until the crisps are starting to brown. Slide the sheet of parchment with the crisps onto another plate. Repeat until all of the cheese is used. Allow the crisps to cool before removing them from the parchment paper.

4. Serve the spread with the Parmesan crisps. Best if eaten the same day.

NET CARBS 3.9g

| calories | fat | protein | carbs | fiber |
|----------|-----|---------|-------|-------|
| 334 | 29.7g | 12.4g | 4.3g | 0.5g |

# Pizza Dip

yield: 8 servings · prep time: 5 minutes · cook time: 25 minutes

1 (8-ounce) package cream cheese, softened

½ cup sour cream

2 cups shredded mozzarella cheese, divided

1 teaspoon dried basil

1 teaspoon ground dried oregano

½ teaspoon garlic powder

½ cup marinara sauce, store-bought or homemade (page 271)

¼ cup pepperoni slices

**Serving Suggestions:**

Cucumber slices

Mini sweet peppers or bell pepper strips

Pork rinds

1. Preheat the oven to 350°F. Grease a 9-inch pie plate.

2. In a medium-size bowl, mix together the cream cheese, sour cream, and 1 cup of the mozzarella until thoroughly combined. Stir in the basil, oregano, and garlic powder.

3. Spread the mixture evenly in the prepared pie plate. Spoon the marinara over the dip and spread into an even layer. Top with the remaining 1 cup of mozzarella and the pepperoni slices.

4. Bake for 25 minutes, or until the dip is bubbling around the edges. Serve with the dippers of your choice. Leftover dip can be stored in an airtight container in the refrigerator for up to 5 days.

*Note: Kids and adults alike will love this dip! You can use another pizza topping of your choice in place of the pepperoni to customize it to your taste.*

NET CARBS 4.2g

| calories | fat | protein | carbs | fiber |
|----------|-----|---------|-------|-------|
| 240 | 21.1g | 8.9g | 4.4g | 0.2g |

# Deviled Ham

yield: 4 servings • prep time: 10 minutes, plus 2 hours to chill

**1 pound cooked ham, coarsely chopped**

**⅓ cup mayonnaise**

**2 ounces cream cheese (¼ cup)**

**2 teaspoons Dijon mustard**

**1 tablespoon sliced green onions, plus more for garnish if desired**

**½ teaspoon paprika**

**½ teaspoon hot sauce**

Serving Suggestions:

**Cheese crisps**

**Cucumber slices**

Pulse the ham in a food processor until it is finely chopped. Add the rest of the ingredients and pulse to combine. Garnish with more green onions, if desired. Chill for at least 2 hours before serving with the scoopers of your choice. Leftovers can be stored in an airtight container in the refrigerator for up to 5 days.

*Note: Deviled ham is a throwback to the 1980s. I say it needs to make a comeback! The canned variety doesn't compare to homemade. It's so easy to prepare and can be served with scoopers, in lettuce wraps, or as a salad topping.*

NET CARBS 1g

| calories | fat | protein | carbs | fiber |
|----------|------|---------|-------|-------|
| 501 | 40.6g | 31.7g | 1.2g | 0.3g |

# Low-Carb Onion Rings

yield: 4 servings • prep time: 15 minutes • cook time: 15 minutes

**High-quality oil, for frying**

**1 large egg**

**1 tablespoon heavy cream**

**1 tablespoon water**

**¼ cup finely crushed pork rinds**

**¼ cup whey protein powder (unflavored and unsweetened)**

**1 teaspoon dried parsley**

**½ teaspoon ground dried oregano**

**½ teaspoon paprika**

**½ teaspoon ground black pepper**

**1 large onion, cut into ¼-inch slices**

**Ketchup (no sugar added), for serving (optional)**

1. Attach a candy thermometer to a 6-quart Dutch oven or similar size heavy pot. Pour in 2 inches of oil and set the pot over medium-high heat. Heat the oil to 350°F.

2. While the oil is heating, beat the egg, cream, and water together in a shallow dish.

3. Put the pork rinds, protein powder, and seasonings in a gallon-size resealable plastic bag or a bowl with a lid. Seal and gently shake.

4. Dip the onion rings in the egg mixture a few at a time, allowing the excess to drip back into the bowl, then place them in the bag with the breading mixture. Seal the bag and shake gently to coat the onion rings. Remove the coated rings from the bag and set aside. Repeat until all of the rings are coated.

5. Working in small batches, fry the onion rings until golden brown on both sides, 2 to 3 minutes per side. Drain on a paper towel–lined plate. Serve immediately with ketchup, if desired.

*Notes: These days it's pretty easy to find low-carb substitutes in restaurants, but I still haven't found one for onion rings. No worries, it's simple to make a lower-carb version of onion rings at home!*

*Do not use an air fryer for this recipe. The whey protein powder requires oil for the correct results.*

## Deep-Frying Tips

For frying, you can use a deep fryer or a large, deep, heavy pot, such as a Dutch oven. A heavy pot helps maintain the temperature of the oil and cook foods evenly, and the depth of the pot keeps messes to a minimum.

When choosing oil for deep-frying, look for a keto-friendly oil with a high smoke point. Avocado oil is an ideal choice.

It's important to maintain a consistent temperature when deep-frying. If the temperature of the oil is too low, the food will absorb the oil and become soggy instead of crispy. I use a candy thermometer to monitor and maintain a consistent temperature. Adding too much food to the oil at one time will lower the temperature quickly; that is why many recipes call for deep-frying foods in batches so as not to overcrowd the pot. When frying in batches, make sure that the oil has returned to the ideal temperature before adding the next batch of food.

NET CARBS 2.7g

| calories | fat | protein | carbs | fiber |
|---|---|---|---|---|
| 101 | 2.7g | 14.7g | 3.7g | 0.9g |

Foods should be completely submerged in the oil when frying. That is why I give the quantity of oil in inches rather than listing a volume amount. This ensures the correct depth of oil for the food being fried, regardless of the diameter of the pot used.

It's important not to overfill the pot with oil so as to avoid a grease fire; a good general rule is never to fill a pot more than halfway full. Watch the oil throughout the cooking process; never walk away from hot oil.

You could use a fresh batch of oil every time, but keto-friendly oils are expensive. Oil used for frying can be reused as long as it's stored properly. Allow the oil to cool completely. Use a mesh skimmer to strain the oil into a container with a lid; a glass jar works well. Store the oil in a cool, dry place. (It does not have to be refrigerated.) If the oil looks cloudy or has a bad smell, it's time to discard it.

# Stuffed Banana Peppers

yield: 4 servings · prep time: 15 minutes · cook time: 24 minutes

**6 large banana peppers**

**1 (8-ounce) package cream cheese, softened**

**1 (4-ounce) can diced green chilies**

**12 thin-cut slices bacon**

1. Preheat the oven to 425°F. Line a sheet pan with parchment paper. Place a broiler rack in the pan.

2. Slice the banana peppers in half lengthwise and remove the seeds. In a small bowl, mix together the cream cheese and chilies until well combined. Fill the pepper halves with the cream cheese mixture, then wrap each one with a slice of bacon. Place on the broiler rack.

3. Bake for 20 minutes. Turn the oven to broil and cook for 2 to 4 more minutes, until the bacon reaches your desired crispness. Allow to sit for 10 minutes before serving. Best if eaten the same day.

*Note: We all love stuffed jalapeños, but have you tried stuffed banana peppers? A banana pepper is milder, but when combined with green chilies, it still has a bit of a kick. And it's wrapped in bacon, so that's a bonus!*

NET CARBS 3.3g

| calories | fat | protein | carbs | fiber |
|----------|------|---------|-------|-------|
| 166 | 12.3g | 5.1g | 6.6g | 3.3g |

# Baked Raspberry Walnut Brie

yield: 8 servings · prep time: 10 minutes (not including time to make jam)
cook time: 15 minutes

**1 recipe Sugar-Free Raspberry Jam (page 274)**

**¼ cup coarsely chopped raw walnuts, plus more for garnish if desired**

**1 tablespoon sugar-free maple syrup**

**1 (16-ounce) wheel Brie**

**Pinch of kosher-size salt**

1. Preheat the oven to 350°F. Line a sheet pan with parchment paper.

2. In a small bowl, mix together the jam, walnuts, and maple syrup. Place the Brie in the prepared pan. Spread the jam mixture evenly over the Brie. Sprinkle with a pinch of kosher salt.

3. Bake for 12 to 15 minutes, until the cheese is starting to melt. Allow to sit for 5 minutes before serving. Garnish with additional walnuts, if desired. Leftovers can be stored in an airtight container in the refrigerator for up to 2 days.

> *Note: This beautiful and tasty appetizer is great served with Parmesan crisps, more nuts, and celery sticks. It would also be a tasty addition to a charcuterie board.*

NET CARBS 1.8g

| calories | fat | protein | carbs | fiber |
|----------|------|---------|-------|-------|
| 242 | 20.9g | 8.9g | 3g | 1.3g |

# Everything Crackers

yield: 6 servings · prep time: 10 minutes · cook time: 15 minutes

**1 cup finely ground blanched almond flour**

**¼ cup whey protein powder (unflavored and unsweetened)**

**¼ teaspoon baking powder**

**1 large egg white**

**1 tablespoon salted butter, melted (not hot)**

**1 teaspoon everything bagel seasoning**

1. Preheat the oven to 350°F.

2. In a medium-size bowl, mix together the almond flour, protein powder, and baking powder.

3. In a small bowl, whisk together the egg white, melted butter, and everything bagel seasoning. Add the egg white mixture to the almond flour mixture, stirring until a cohesive dough forms.

4. Place the dough on a piece of parchment paper. Top it with another piece of parchment and use a rolling pin to roll out the dough to about a ⅛-inch thickness.

5. Remove the top piece of parchment paper and use a pizza cutter to cut the dough into 2-inch crackers. Spread them about 1 inch apart, then carefully slide the parchment paper with the crackers onto a baking sheet.

6. Bake for 15 minutes, or until the crackers start to brown around the edges. Let the crackers cool completely on the pan before serving. They will crisp more as they cool. Store in an airtight container for up to a week.

*Note: These crackers can be used anytime a low-carb cracker is needed. The whey in this recipe helps give the crackers a little more crunch than ordinary almond flour crackers. You can easily change the flavor profile by substituting your favorite spice or herb blend for the everything bagel seasoning.*

NET CARBS 1.9g

| calories | fat | protein | carbs | fiber |
|----------|------|---------|-------|-------|
| 136 | 10.9g | 7.6g | 3.6g | 1.8g |

# Crispy Buffalo Shrimp

yield: 4 servings • prep time: 15 minutes • cook time: 10 minutes

1 pound medium shrimp, peeled and deveined

2 tablespoons coconut flour

1 large egg

1 tablespoon heavy cream

½ cup whey protein powder (unflavored and unsweetened)

¼ teaspoon salt

¼ teaspoon ground black pepper

¼ teaspoon garlic powder

¼ teaspoon onion powder

¼ teaspoon paprika

High-quality oil, for frying

¼ cup Buffalo sauce, store-bought or homemade (page 273)

Serving Suggestions:

Ranch Dressing (page 268)

Celery sticks

1. Make sure the shrimp are dry. Use paper towels to remove any excess moisture.

2. Place the coconut flour in a shallow dish.

3. In a small bowl, whisk together the egg and cream.

4. In another shallow dish, stir together the protein powder, salt, and spices.

5. Attach a candy thermometer to a 6-quart Dutch oven or similar-size heavy pot. Pour in 2 inches of oil and set the pot over medium-high heat. Heat the oil to 350°F.

6. Working in small batches, lightly dust the shrimp in the coconut flour, then dip them in the egg mixture, allowing the excess to drip back into the bowl. Finally, dredge the shrimp in the seasoned protein powder. Put the coated shrimp on a plate. Repeat until all of the shrimp are coated.

7. Fry the shrimp in batches until light golden brown. This should take only 2 to 3 minutes per batch. Drain the shrimp on a paper towel–lined plate.

8. Gently toss the shrimp in the Buffalo sauce. Serve with celery sticks and ranch dressing, if desired.

NET CARBS 1g

| calories | fat | protein | carbs | fiber |
|---|---|---|---|---|
| 181 | 3.7g | 33.4g | 2.3g | 1.3g |

# Pecan-Encrusted Tuna Ball

yield: 8 servings • prep time: 15 minutes, plus overnight to chill

**2 (8-ounce) packages cream cheese, softened**

**1 (5-ounce) can tuna, drained**

**¼ cup thinly sliced green onions**

**½ cup shredded cheddar cheese**

**1 cup chopped raw pecans, divided**

**Serving Suggestions:**

**Celery sticks**

**Low-carb crackers (such as the Everything Crackers on page 92)**

**Mini sweet peppers or bell pepper strips**

**Pork rinds**

1. In a medium-size mixing bowl, stir together the cream cheese, tuna, green onions, cheddar cheese, and ½ cup of the pecans until well blended.

2. Shape the mixture into a ball and roll it in the remaining pecans. Wrap the ball in plastic wrap and refrigerate overnight before serving.

3. Serve with the scoopers of your choice. Leftovers can be stored in an airtight container in the refrigerator for up to 5 days.

NET CARBS 2.7g

| calories | fat | protein | carbs | fiber |
|---|---|---|---|---|
| 279 | 25g | 11g | 3.2g | 0.5g |

# Spicy Ranch Dip

yield: 6 servings • prep time: 5 minutes, plus 2 hours to chill

½ cup sour cream

½ cup mayonnaise

1 jalapeño pepper, seeded and finely chopped

½ teaspoon salt

½ teaspoon snipped fresh chives

½ teaspoon dried dill weed

½ teaspoon dried parsley

½ teaspoon ground cumin

½ teaspoon smoked paprika

¼ teaspoon garlic powder

¼ teaspoon onion powder

¼ teaspoon ground black pepper

**Serving Suggestions:**

Celery sticks

Cucumber slices

Low-carb crackers (such as the Everything Crackers on page 92)

Mini sweet peppers or bell pepper strips

Pork rinds

In a small mixing bowl, mix all of the ingredients thoroughly. Put in the refrigerator to chill for at least 2 hours before serving with the scoopers of your choice. Leftover dip can be stored in an airtight container in the refrigerator for up to a week.

NET CARBS 1.4g

| calories | fat | protein | carbs | fiber |
|----------|-----|---------|-------|-------|
| 177 | 19g | 0.8g | 1.7g | 0.3g |

# Roasted Red Pepper Hummus

yield: 6 servings • prep time: 10 minutes, plus 1 hour optional chilling time

cook time: 25 minutes

**1 medium head cauliflower, cut into florets**

**1 red bell pepper, seeded and quartered**

**4 tablespoons extra-virgin olive oil, divided, plus more for drizzling**

**Salt and pepper**

**2 tablespoons natural almond butter**

**2 tablespoons freshly squeezed lemon juice**

**1 clove garlic, peeled**

**½ teaspoon ground cumin**

**½ teaspoon smoked paprika**

Serving Suggestions:

**Cucumber slices**

**Pork rinds**

**Radish slices**

1. Preheat the oven to 425°F. Line a sheet pan with parchment paper.

2. In a medium-size bowl, toss the cauliflower florets and red bell pepper quarters with 2 tablespoons of the olive oil and a pinch each of salt and pepper. Spread evenly across the prepared sheet pan. Roast for 20 to 25 minutes, until the cauliflower is tender and the pepper is charred and fragrant.

3. Peel off and discard the charred pepper skin. Place the cauliflower and bell pepper in a food processor. Add the almond butter, lemon juice, garlic, cumin, paprika, and the remaining 2 tablespoons of olive oil and process until blended and smooth. Transfer to a serving bowl and chill for 1 hour, if desired, or serve immediately.

4. Drizzle with a small amount of olive oil and serve with the dippers of your choice. Leftovers can be stored in an airtight container in the refrigerator for up to 5 days.

*Note: When I started following a keto lifestyle, I missed hummus badly. Roasted red pepper was always my favorite flavor. You will not miss the chickpeas in this hummus; it's delicious!*

NET CARBS 4.5g

| calories | fat | protein | carbs | fiber |
|----------|-----|---------|-------|-------|
| 148 | 12.1g | 3.2g | 7.7g | 3.2g |

# Sweet & Salty Snack Mix

yield: 2 cups (¼ cup per serving) · prep time: 10 minutes · cook time: 8 minutes

**1 tablespoon salted butter**

**1 cup raw almonds or pecan halves**

**¼ cup roasted peanuts**

**¼ cup roasted and salted shelled pumpkin seeds**

**¼ cup roasted and salted shelled sunflower seeds**

**¼ cup unsweetened coconut flakes**

**¼ cup sugar-free chocolate chips and/or white chocolate chips**

1. Preheat the oven to 350°F. Line a sheet pan with parchment paper.

2. In a medium-size microwave-safe bowl, microwave the butter until melted, stirring every 10 seconds. Add the almonds to the bowl and stir until the nuts are coated. Spread the almonds evenly in the prepared pan.

3. Bake for 7 to 8 minutes, or until fragrant, stirring halfway through. Transfer the almonds to a large mixing bowl; allow to cool completely.

4. To the bowl with the almonds, add the peanuts, pumpkin seeds, sunflower seeds, coconut, and chocolate chips and toss to combine. Leftovers can be stored in an airtight container for up to 2 weeks.

*Note: This recipe is easy to customize by using different nuts and seeds. You can also try different types of chocolate chips—all regular chocolate chips, all white, or a combination.*

NET CARBS 3.4g

| calories | fat | protein | carbs | fiber |
|----------|-----|---------|-------|-------|
| 235 | 20.6g | 7g | 10.4g | 7g |

#  Soups & Salads

# Maple Dijon Broccoli Slaw

yield: 6 servings • prep time: 5 minutes, plus 2 hours to chill

**Dressing:**

¼ cup avocado oil

3 tablespoons sugar-free maple syrup

1 tablespoon Dijon mustard

1 tablespoon apple cider vinegar

½ teaspoon salt

½ teaspoon ground black pepper

1 drop liquid stevia

1 (12-ounce) bag broccoli slaw

¼ cup sliced almonds, plus more for garnish

Toasted sesame seeds, for garnish

Freshly ground black pepper, for garnish

1. In a medium-size serving bowl, whisk together all of the dressing ingredients.

2. Add the broccoli slaw and almonds to the bowl and toss until well coated with the dressing. Refrigerate for at least 2 hours before serving.

3. Garnish the slaw with sliced almonds, toasted sesame seeds, and freshly ground pepper and serve. Leftovers can be stored in an airtight container in the refrigerator for up to 3 days.

NET CARBS 2.7g

| calories | fat | protein | carbs | fiber |
|----------|-----|---------|-------|-------|
| 140 | 11.5g | 2.3g | 4.5g | 2g |

# Strawberry Spinach Salad

yield: 4 servings • prep time: 15 minutes (not including time to make dressing)

**4 cups baby spinach**

**½ cup thinly sliced red onions**

**1 cup halved or sliced strawberries**

**¼ cup sliced almonds**

**8 slices bacon, cooked and crumbled**

**1 recipe Poppy Seed Dressing (page 269)**

In a large serving bowl, layer all of the salad ingredients, starting with the spinach and ending with the bacon. When ready to serve, add the dressing and gently toss. Best if eaten the same day.

NET CARBS 5g

| calories | fat | protein | carbs | fiber |
|---|---|---|---|---|
| 306 | 28.1g | 9.4g | 10.7g | 5.7g |

# Asian Coleslaw

yield: 4 servings • prep time: 5 minutes, plus 2 hours to chill

1 (10-ounce) bag tri-color coleslaw

1 green onion, thinly sliced

Dressing:

¼ cup coarsely chopped roasted peanuts

¼ cup white vinegar

3 tablespoons extra-virgin olive oil

2 tablespoons brown sugar substitute

1 tablespoon coconut aminos

1 tablespoon toasted sesame oil

1 tablespoon ginger powder

2 teaspoons toasted sesame seeds

1 clove garlic, minced

½ teaspoon salt

½ teaspoon ground black pepper

1. In a medium-size serving bowl, toss the coleslaw and green onion.

2. In a small bowl, whisk together all of the dressing ingredients.

3. Drizzle the dressing over the slaw and gently toss to combine. Chill for at least 2 hours before serving. Leftovers can be stored in an airtight container in the refrigerator for up to 5 days.

NET CARBS 5.5g

| calories | fat | protein | carbs | fiber |
|----------|-----|---------|-------|-------|
| 239 | 22.2g | 4.5g | 8.7g | 3.5g |

# Layered Summer Salad

yield: 6 servings • prep time: 20 minutes, plus 6 hours to chill

**3 hearts romaine lettuce, chopped into bite-size pieces**

**6 mini sweet peppers (any color), sliced**

**3 mini cucumbers, sliced**

**½ red onion, diced, divided**

**½ cup finely chopped celery**

**4 hard-boiled eggs, halved or sliced**

**1 pint cherry tomatoes**

**1 cup shredded cheddar cheese**

**10 slices bacon, cooked and crumbled**

Dressing:

**¾ cup sour cream**

**½ cup mayonnaise**

**1 tablespoon granular sweetener**

**½ teaspoon ground black pepper**

1. Arrange the lettuce in an even layer in a trifle bowl or other large glass serving bowl. Layer the sweet peppers, cucumbers, most of the red onion, the celery, eggs, and tomatoes on top of the lettuce.

2. In a small bowl, whisk together all of the dressing ingredients.

3. Spread the dressing evenly over the salad, spreading it all the way to the edge of the bowl. Top with the cheese, bacon, and remaining red onion. Cover and refrigerate for at least 6 hours or overnight for the best flavor.

4. Toss to combine all of the salad ingredients with the dressing before serving. Best if eaten the same day, but leftovers can be stored in an airtight container in the refrigerator for up to 2 days.

*Note: I remember eating this old-fashioned salad at summer gatherings growing up. The ingredients are simple but wonderful when stirred together after the salad is chilled.*

NET CARBS 4.9g

| calories | fat | protein | carbs | fiber |
|---|---|---|---|---|
| 354 | 28g | 15.7g | 6.7g | 1.8g |

# Antipasto Salad with Creamy Italian Dressing

yield: 8 servings · prep time: 15 minutes

**2 hearts romaine lettuce, chopped into bite-size pieces**

**1 (7.5-ounce) jar quartered marinated artichoke hearts**

**1 (6-ounce) can pitted black olives**

**1 cup mini pepperoni slices**

**1 cup sliced salami**

**½ cup banana pepper rings**

**¼ cup chopped sun-dried tomatoes (oil-packed)**

**1 cup fresh mini mozzarella balls, cut in half**

**Dressing:**

**½ cup mayonnaise**

**⅓ cup white vinegar**

**¼ cup grated Parmesan cheese**

**1 tablespoon extra-virgin olive oil**

**1 tablespoon freshly squeezed lemon juice**

**2 teaspoons Italian seasoning**

**1 teaspoon granular sweetener**

**½ teaspoon dried parsley**

**½ teaspoon salt**

**½ teaspoon ground black pepper**

1. Place the lettuce in a large serving bowl. Arrange the rest of the salad ingredients on top of the lettuce.

2. In a small bowl, whisk together all of the dressing ingredients.

3. Drizzle the dressing over the salad. Gently toss until all of the salad ingredients are coated with the dressing. Serve immediately. Leftovers can be stored in an airtight container in the refrigerator for up to 3 days.

*Note: This salad is so hearty and delicious. The flavorful dressing is my take on Olive Garden's house dressing. You can use regular-size pepperoni slices in place of the minis; the minis are just my preference.*

NET CARBS 5.2g

| calories | fat | protein | carbs | fiber |
|----------|------|---------|-------|-------|
| 408 | 35.8g | 13.2g | 8.7g | 3.5g |

# Zuppa Toscana

yield: 6 servings • prep time: 10 minutes • cook time: 45 minutes

1 pound bulk Italian sausage

4 slices bacon, chopped

½ cup finely chopped onions

2 cloves garlic, minced

3 cups vegetable broth

12 ounces frozen cauliflower florets

1 (10-ounce) package frozen leaf spinach

2 teaspoons Italian seasoning

1 cup heavy cream

Salt and pepper

Shredded Parmesan cheese, for garnish (optional)

Red pepper flakes, for garnish (optional)

1. Put the sausage, bacon, onions, and garlic in a stockpot over medium heat. Cook, crumbling the sausage with a large spoon, until the meats are browned, about 10 minutes. Drain any excess fat.

2. Add the broth, cauliflower, spinach, and Italian seasoning to the pot. Bring to a low boil and cook until the cauliflower is tender, about 15 minutes.

3. Reduce the heat to low and stir in the cream. Simmer the soup for 15 more minutes, stirring often. Season with salt and pepper to taste.

4. Serve garnished with Parmesan cheese and red pepper flakes, if desired. Leftovers can be stored in an airtight container in the refrigerator for up to 5 days.

*Note: This is my favorite restaurant-style Italian soup! I've been making it for years. Before keto, I made it with potatoes. I also prefer the flavor of spinach over kale, which is what's normally used.*

NET CARBS 6.6g

| calories | fat | protein | carbs | fiber |
|----------|-----|---------|-------|-------|
| 376 | 29.2g | 18.3g | 9.9g | 3.3g |

# Unstuffed Pepper Soup

option

yield: 8 servings • prep time: 10 minutes • cook time: 45 minutes

**1 pound bulk breakfast sausage**

**1 (12-ounce) bag frozen bell pepper and onion blend**

**2 cloves garlic, minced**

**2 cups vegetable broth**

**1½ cups marinara sauce, store-bought or homemade (page 271)**

**1 (14.5-ounce) can petite diced tomatoes**

**1 (10-ounce) bag frozen riced cauliflower**

**1 teaspoon dried basil**

**1 teaspoon ground dried oregano**

**½ teaspoon salt**

**½ teaspoon ground black pepper**

For Garnish (Optional):

**Chopped fresh parsley**

**Shredded cheese of choice**

1. Put the sausage and pepper and onion blend in a stockpot over medium heat. Cook, crumbling the sausage with a large spoon, until the meat is browned and the vegetables are tender, about 10 minutes. Add the garlic and cook for 1 more minute. Drain any excess fat.

2. Add the broth, marinara, tomatoes, riced cauliflower, basil, oregano, salt, and black pepper to the pot. Bring to a boil, then lower the heat to maintain a low boil; cook until the cauliflower is tender, about 10 minutes. Reduce the heat to low and simmer for 20 minutes to allow the flavors to develop.

3. Serve garnished with parsley and shredded cheese, if desired. Leftovers can be stored in an airtight container in the refrigerator for up to 5 days.

NET CARBS 8.5g

| calories | fat | protein | carbs | fiber |
|---|---|---|---|---|
| 251 | 19.3g | 14.1g | 10.5g | 2g |

# French Onion Soup

yield: 6 servings • prep time: 10 minutes • cook time: 55 minutes

¼ cup (½ stick) salted butter

4 small onions, thinly sliced

2 cloves garlic, minced

½ cup dry white wine

4 cups beef broth

1 tablespoon Worcestershire sauce

½ teaspoon xanthan gum

1 bay leaf

Salt and pepper

1½ cups shredded Gruyère cheese

**Bread Toppers:**

3 tablespoons salted butter, divided

9 tablespoons finely ground blanched almond flour, divided

3 large eggs, divided

¾ teaspoon baking powder, divided

1. In a 6-quart Dutch oven or a stockpot, melt the butter over medium heat. Add the onions and cook until caramelized, about 30 minutes. Stir them every few minutes. Toward the end of cooking, stir them often; be careful not to burn them. They should be golden brown.

2. Add the garlic and cook for 1 minute. Stir in the wine to deglaze the pot. Use a spoon to scrape the bits off the bottom of the pot.

3. Stir in the broth, Worcestershire, xanthan gum, and bay leaf. Allow the soup to reach a low boil, then lower the heat and simmer until the soup thickens slightly, about 15 more minutes.

4. Meanwhile, make the bread toppers: Have on hand three 8-ounce microwave-safe ramekins. Put 1 tablespoon of butter in one of the ramekins and heat in the microwave until just melted. Stir in 3 tablespoons of the almond flour, 1 egg, and ¼ teaspoon of the baking powder until well combined. Microwave for 1 minute. Check it and add 15 seconds as needed until the topper is set and fully cooked. Set aside to cool. Repeat with the remaining ingredients and other two ramekins. When the toppers are completely cool, turn them out and slice in half horizontally to make a total of 6 round pieces of bread.

5. When the soup is done, remove the bay leaf and season the soup with salt and pepper to taste.

6. Ladle the soup into six individual-size ovenproof serving bowls. Place a bread topper in each bowl and top with a generous amount of cheese. Place the bowls on a sheet pan.

7. Place an oven rack in the top position, then turn the oven to the broil setting. Place the pan under the broiler to toast the bread and melt the cheese, 2 to 4 minutes. Watch closely so they don't burn. Serve immediately. Leftovers can be stored in an airtight container in the refrigerator for up to 5 days.

NET CARBS 5.3g

| calories | fat | protein | carbs | fiber |
|---|---|---|---|---|
| 387 | 26.8g | 16.6g | 7g | 1.7g |

# Green Chile Chicken Soup

yield: 6 servings • prep time: 10 minutes • cook time: 55 minutes

**2 tablespoons avocado oil**

**¼ cup finely chopped onions**

**1 jalapeño pepper, seeded and chopped**

**2 cloves garlic, minced**

**1 pound boneless, skinless chicken thighs**

**4 cups chicken broth**

**1 (4-ounce) can diced green chilies**

**2 teaspoons ground cumin**

**Salt and pepper**

**1 cup sour cream**

### Suggested Garnishes:

**Shredded Mexican cheese blend**

**Sliced jalapeño peppers**

**Fresh cilantro leaves**

1. Heat the oil in a stockpot over medium heat. Add the onions and chopped jalapeño and cook, stirring often, until tender, about 10 minutes. Stir in the garlic and cook for 1 more minute.

2. Add the chicken to the pot and cook on both sides until no longer pink in the center, about 20 minutes. Use two forks to shred the chicken in the pot.

3. Stir in the broth, chilies, and cumin. Bring the soup to a low boil and continue to cook for 20 minutes. Remove the pot from the heat and season the soup with salt and pepper to taste. Stir in the sour cream.

4. Serve garnished with shredded cheese, sliced jalapeños, and/ or cilantro leaves, if desired. Leftovers can be stored in an airtight container in the refrigerator for up to 5 days.

NET CARBS 4g

| calories | fat | protein | carbs | fiber |
|----------|-----|---------|-------|-------|
| 246 | 15.9g | 19.5g | 5g | 1g |

# Easy Buffalo Chicken Soup

yield: 4 servings • prep time: 10 minutes • cook time: 35 minutes

2 tablespoons avocado oil

½ cup chopped celery

¼ cup finely chopped onions

2 cloves garlic, minced

3 cups shredded rotisserie chicken

4 ounces cream cheese (½ cup), softened

3 cups chicken broth

¼ cup Buffalo sauce, store-bought or homemade (page 273)

2 teaspoons dried parsley

1 teaspoon dried chives

Salt and pepper

**Suggested Toppings:**

Shredded Monterey Jack cheese or cheddar cheese, or crumbed blue cheese

Sliced green onions or snipped fresh chives

Cooked and crumbled bacon

1. Heat the oil in a stockpot over medium heat. Add the celery and onions and cook, stirring often, until tender, about 10 minutes. Add the garlic and cook for 1 more minute.

2. Add the chicken and cream cheese to the pot. Stir until the cream cheese is melted.

3. Add the broth, Buffalo sauce, parsley, and chives. Bring the soup to a low boil while stirring frequently, then reduce the heat to low. Continue to simmer for 20 more minutes to allow the flavors to develop. Season the soup with salt and pepper to taste.

4. Serve with the toppings of your choice. Leftovers can be stored in an airtight container in the refrigerator for up to 5 days.

NET CARBS 2.8g

| calories | fat | protein | carbs | fiber |
|----------|-----|---------|-------|-------|
| 401 | 15.4g | 38.2g | 3.3g | 0.5g |

# Sheet Pan Zucchini Pizza Bake

yield: 6 servings · prep time: 10 minutes · cook time: 23 minutes

**2 medium zucchini, sliced**

**2 tablespoons avocado oil**

**¼ teaspoon garlic salt**

**½ cup marinara sauce, store-bought or homemade (page 271)**

**1 cup shredded mozzarella cheese**

**½ cup ricotta cheese**

**½ cup pepperoni slices**

1. Preheat the oven to 400°F. Line a sheet pan with parchment paper.

2. Toss the zucchini slices in the oil until evenly coated. Place them in the prepared pan in a single layer. Sprinkle with the garlic salt. Bake for 20 minutes, or until tender and brown around the edges. Remove from the oven and turn the oven to broil.

3. Top the zucchini with the marinara, mozzarella, spoonfuls of the ricotta, and the pepperoni. Broil for 2 to 3 minutes, or until the toppings start to brown. Watch closely so as not to let it burn. Serve immediately.

NET CARBS 2.9g

| calories | fat | protein | carbs | fiber |
|----------|-----|---------|-------|-------|
| 157 | 12.6g | 7.5g | 4.1g | 1.2g |

# Salisbury Steak

yield: 4 servings • prep time: 10 minutes • cook time: 30 minutes

1 pound ground beef

1 large egg

1 teaspoon Worcestershire sauce

½ teaspoon onion powder

½ teaspoon ground black pepper

2 tablespoons salted butter

1 small onion, sliced

1 cup sliced mushrooms

1 clove garlic, minced

1 cup beef broth

½ cup heavy cream

½ teaspoon xanthan gum

Chopped fresh parsley, for garnish

1. Put the ground beef, egg, Worcestershire, onion powder, and pepper in a medium-size mixing bowl. Mix with your hands just until combined; do not overmix. Shape into 4 patties about 1 inch thick.

2. Heat the butter in a large skillet over medium heat. Put the onion slices in the skillet and cook for 5 minutes, then add the mushrooms and garlic. Continue cooking until the mushrooms are tender, about 5 minutes. Remove the mushroom mixture from the skillet and set aside.

3. Place the patties in the skillet and cook until browned on both sides, about 5 minutes per side. Return the mushroom mixture to the skillet. Stir in the broth, cream, and xanthan gum. Continue cooking until the patties are cooked through and the gravy thickens, about 10 minutes. Garnish with parsley. Leftovers can be stored in an airtight container in the refrigerator for up to 5 days.

NET CARBS 2.3g

| calories | fat | protein | carbs | fiber |
|----------|-----|---------|-------|-------|
| 483 | 40.5g | 23.9g | 3.6g | 1.6g |

# Sheet Pan Smoked Sausage & Cabbage

yield: 4 servings · prep time: 10 minutes · cook time: 25 minutes

½ head red cabbage, shredded

½ head green cabbage, shredded

2 tablespoons avocado oil

Salt and pepper

12 ounces smoked rope sausage, sliced

1. Preheat the oven to 400°F. Line a sheet pan with parchment paper.

2. Toss the shredded cabbages with the oil until completely coated. Season with salt and pepper. Spread out in the prepared pan.

3. Bake for 15 minutes, then remove from the oven and give it a stir. Add the sausage slices to the cabbages and return the pan to the oven. Cook until the sausage is browned, 5 to 10 more minutes. Leftovers can be stored in an airtight container in the refrigerator for up to 3 days.

NET CARBS 6.9g

| calories | fat | protein | carbs | fiber |
|----------|-----|---------|-------|-------|
| 369 | 32.7g | 10.8g | 10.2g | 3.4g |

# Country Fried Steak & Gravy

yield: 4 servings • prep time: 10 minutes • cook time: 20 minutes

1 large egg, whisked

¾ cup finely crushed pork rinds

¼ cup whey protein powder (unflavored and unsweetened)

½ teaspoon ground black pepper

½ teaspoon smoked paprika

½ teaspoon garlic powder

¼ teaspoon onion powder

¼ teaspoon salt

4 (4-ounce) cube steaks

2 tablespoons avocado oil

2 tablespoons salted butter

Gravy:

¾ cup heavy cream

½ cup water

¼ teaspoon xanthan gum

Salt and pepper

1. Set up two dipping stations in two shallow bowls: Put the egg in one bowl, and combine the pork rinds, protein powder, spices, and salt in the other bowl.

2. Dip both sides of a steak in the egg, allowing the excess to drip back into the bowl, then place the steak in the pork rind mixture, pressing it on both sides. Repeat until all of the steaks are coated.

3. In a large skillet over medium heat, heat the oil and butter until melted. Fry the steaks until golden brown, 3 to 4 minutes on each side. Remove from the pan and set aside. Cover to keep warm.

4. To make the gravy, reduce the heat to low. To the drippings, add the cream, water, and xanthan gum. Cook, stirring frequently, until the gravy starts to thicken, about 10 minutes. Season the gravy with salt and pepper to taste.

5. Serve the gravy over the steaks. Best if eaten the same day.

NET CARBS 0.7g

| calories | fat | protein | carbs | fiber |
|----------|-----|---------|-------|-------|
| 551 | 42g | 35.3g | 1g | 0.5g |

# Garlic Parmesan Shrimp

yield: 4 servings • prep time: 5 minutes • cook time: 10 minutes

**1 pound medium shrimp, peeled and deveined**

**2 tablespoons salted butter, melted**

**2 cloves garlic, minced**

**¼ cup minced fresh basil**

**1 teaspoon dried parsley**

**½ teaspoon ground dried oregano**

**½ cup shredded Parmesan cheese**

**Kosher-size salt**

**Freshly ground black pepper**

**Red pepper flakes**

1. Place an oven rack in the middle position and preheat the oven to 400°F. Line a sheet pan with parchment paper.

2. Pat the shrimp dry. Place in a bowl and toss with the melted butter, garlic, basil, parsley, and oregano. Spread out the shrimp in the prepared pan and bake for 8 minutes, until pink. Remove the pan from the oven.

3. Turn the oven to broil. Top the shrimp with the Parmesan cheese, then return the pan to the middle rack and broil for 1 to 2 minutes, until the cheese is melted.

4. Sprinkle with salt, black pepper, and red pepper flakes and serve immediately.

NET CARBS 1.9g

| calories | fat | protein | carbs | fiber |
|----------|-----|---------|-------|-------|
| 196 | 9g | 23.1g | 2.1g | 0.2g |

# Zucchini Parmesan

yield: 4 servings • prep time: 20 minutes • cook time: 40 minutes

**2 large eggs**

**1 tablespoon heavy cream**

**1 cup finely crushed pork rinds**

**1 cup grated Parmesan cheese**

**2 teaspoons Italian seasoning**

**2 medium zucchini, sliced**

**1 cup marinara sauce, store-bought or homemade (page 271), divided**

**1 cup shredded mozzarella cheese, divided**

**Chopped fresh basil leaves, for garnish**

1. Preheat the oven to 425°F. Line a sheet pan with parchment paper. Grease an 8 by 11-inch baking pan.

2. In a shallow dish, whisk together the eggs and cream. In another shallow dish, use a fork to combine the pork rinds, Parmesan cheese, and Italian seasoning.

3. Working in small batches, dip the zucchini slices into the egg wash and then into the pork rind mixture, gently pressing the crumbs onto both sides of the zucchini.

4. Place the coated zucchini slices on the prepared sheet pan and bake for 15 minutes, then remove from the oven and flip the slices over. Bake for 10 more minutes. Both sides should be golden brown.

5. Spread ½ cup of the marinara evenly over the bottom of the prepared baking pan. Place half of the baked zucchini in an even layer across the bottom of the pan. Spread the rest of the marinara evenly over the zucchini. Sprinkle ½ cup of the mozzarella evenly over the sauce. Layer the rest of the zucchini slices and top with the remaining mozzarella.

6. Bake for 15 minutes, or until the cheese is melted and the sauce is bubbly around the edges. Garnish with fresh basil and serve immediately. Leftovers can be stored in an airtight container in the refrigerator for up to 3 days.

*Note: I created this recipe for my eggplant-loathing husband. He's generally not picky, but he will not eat eggplant, and I like eggplant Parmesan. I got the idea to make a similar dish using zucchini. I actually like this version better!*

NET CARBS 4.7g

| calories | fat | protein | carbs | fiber |
|----------|-----|---------|-------|-------|
| 333 | 20.2g | 28.5g | 6.7g | 2g |

# Meatball Marinara

yield: 6 servings · prep time: 15 minutes · cook time: 40 minutes

**1 pound bulk breakfast sausage**

**1 pound ground beef**

**1 large egg**

**½ teaspoon dried basil, plus more for garnish**

**½ teaspoon dried parsley**

**¼ teaspoon ground dried oregano**

**¼ teaspoon garlic powder**

**¼ teaspoon onion powder**

**¼ teaspoon salt**

**¼ teaspoon ground black pepper**

**1 cup grated Parmesan cheese**

**1½ cups marinara sauce, store-bought or homemade (page 271)**

**1 cup shredded mozzarella cheese**

**1 cup shredded provolone cheese, or 6 slices provolone cheese**

1. Preheat the oven to 400°F. Line a sheet pan with parchment paper. Grease a 2-quart baking dish.

2. In a large bowl, use your hands to gently combine the sausage and ground beef. In a smaller bowl, whisk together the egg and seasonings. Pour the egg mixture over the meat and sprinkle with the Parmesan cheese. Use your hands to gently mix until well combined; be careful not to overwork the meat.

3. Lightly roll the meat mixture into 1½-inch balls and place on the prepared sheet pan. Bake the meatballs for 20 to 25 minutes, until lightly browned.

4. Lower the oven temperature to 375°F. Transfer the meatballs to the prepared baking dish. Top with the marinara, mozzarella, and provolone.

5. Bake for 15 more minutes, or until the cheese is melted and the sauce is bubbly around the edges. Allow to sit for 10 minutes before serving. Garnish with extra basil. Leftovers can be stored in an airtight container in the refrigerator for up to 5 days.

*Note: These meatballs are delicious by themselves or served with a side of zucchini noodles.*

NET CARBS 4.9g

| calories | fat | protein | carbs | fiber |
|---|---|---|---|---|
| 642 | 47.6g | 42.5g | 5.6g | 0.6g |

# Shepherd's Pie

yield: 6 servings · prep time: 20 minutes · cook time: 50 minutes

2 tablespoons avocado oil

½ cup sliced mushrooms

¼ cup chopped onions

2 cloves garlic, minced

2 slices bacon, chopped

1½ pounds ground beef

1 cup tomato sauce

¼ cup beef broth

1 tablespoon Worcestershire sauce

½ teaspoon ground black pepper

1 (16-ounce) bag frozen cauliflower florets

2 tablespoons heavy cream

2 tablespoons salted butter

Salt

½ cup shredded cheddar cheese

Chopped fresh chives, for garnish

1. Preheat the oven to 350°F.

2. Heat the oil in a medium-size cast-iron or other ovenproof skillet over medium heat. Add the mushrooms and onions and stir to coat in the oil. Cook until the vegetables are tender and the onions start to caramelize, about 10 minutes. Stir in the garlic and cook for 1 more minute.

3. Add the bacon and ground beef to the skillet, crumbling the beef as it cooks. Cook until the beef is no longer pink. Add the tomato sauce, broth, Worcestershire, and pepper to the beef mixture. Simmer until the liquid starts to cook down and the mixture is slightly thickened, about 15 minutes, then remove the pan from the heat.

4. Meanwhile, steam the cauliflower according to the package directions. Make sure the cauliflower is fall-apart tender. Drain the excess liquid.

5. Place the cauliflower in a food processor or high-powered blender. Add the cream and butter and pulse until the mixture is smooth and creamy. Season with salt and pepper to taste.

6. Spread the mashed cauliflower evenly over the beef mixture and top with the cheese. Bake for 20 to 25 minutes, until heated through and the cheese is melted. Garnish with chives and serve immediately. Leftovers can be stored in an airtight container in the refrigerator for up to 5 days.

*Note: This comforting dish is traditionally made with lamb, but I prefer beef, the way my mom always made it. The cauli-mash is a wonderful alternative to the potatoes normally found in shepherd's pie.*

NET CARBS 5.2g

| calories | fat | protein | carbs | fiber |
|---|---|---|---|---|
| 466 | 36.6g | 26.3g | 7.9g | 2.8g |

# Ground Beef Teriyaki Bowl

yield: 4 servings • prep time: 5 minutes • cook time: 25 minutes

1 tablespoon toasted sesame oil

1 pound ground beef

4 cloves garlic, minced

1 tablespoon ginger powder

¼ cup brown sugar substitute

¼ cup coconut aminos or gluten-free soy sauce

2 tablespoons sugar-free maple syrup

1 tablespoon unseasoned rice vinegar

2 cups cooked cauliflower rice or steamed broccoli florets, for serving

For Garnish (Optional):

Toasted sesame seeds

Sliced green onions

1. Heat the oil in a large deep skillet or sauté pan over medium heat. Brown the ground beef in the skillet, crumbling the meat as it cooks, about 10 minutes. Add the garlic and ginger powder and cook for 1 to 2 more minutes, until fragrant. Drain any excess fat.

2. Stir in the brown sugar substitute, aminos, maple syrup, and vinegar. Continue cooking, stirring frequently, until the mixture thickens, about 10 minutes.

3. Serve over cauliflower rice or steamed broccoli. Garnish with sesame seeds and green onions, if desired. Leftovers can be stored in an airtight container in the refrigerator for up to 5 days.

*Note: Look for rice vinegar described as "natural" or "all-natural" on the label to avoid the sugar and salt that is included in seasoned rice vinegar.*

NET CARBS 3.4g

| calories | fat | protein | carbs | fiber |
|----------|-----|---------|-------|-------|
| 359 | 26.6g | 22.2g | 4.2g | 0.8g |

# Shrimp Alfredo Spaghetti Squash

yield: 6 servings • prep time: 15 minutes • cook time: 1 hour 5 minutes

**1 small spaghetti squash (about 3 pounds)**

**2 tablespoons avocado oil**

**Pinch of salt**

**Pinch of ground black pepper**

**2 tablespoons salted butter**

**2 cloves garlic, minced**

**1 pound medium shrimp, peeled and deveined**

**½ cup heavy cream**

**1 cup grated Parmesan cheese**

**½ cup shredded Parmesan cheese**

**½ teaspoon red pepper flakes**

**Chopped fresh parsley, for garnish**

1. Preheat the oven to 400°F. Line a sheet pan with parchment paper.

2. Use a knife to pierce holes down both sides of the squash. Microwave the squash for 5 minutes. Carefully remove the squash from the microwave; it will be hot.

3. Cut the squash in half lengthwise. Use a spoon to scoop out the seeds.

4. Drizzle the cut halves of the squash with the oil and sprinkle evenly with the salt and pepper. Place the halves cut side down in the prepared pan and place in the oven. Roast for 35 to 45 minutes, until tender. Use a fork to shred the squash, leaving it in the skin.

5. Melt the butter in a medium-size skillet over medium heat. Add the garlic and shrimp. Cook until the shrimp turns pink, 4 to 5 minutes. Reduce the heat to low. Stir in the cream and grated Parmesan cheese. Cook for 5 more minutes, stirring frequently. Remove from the heat. Turn the oven to broil.

6. Evenly top the squash halves with the shrimp Alfredo mixture. Top with the shredded Parmesan cheese and red pepper flakes. Broil for 2 to 4 minutes, just long enough to melt the cheese and brown the edges. Garnish with fresh parsley and serve immediately.

NET CARBS 5.3g

| calories | fat | protein | carbs | fiber |
|---|---|---|---|---|
| 349 | 31.5g | 11.2g | 6.4g | 1.1g |

# Lump Crab Cakes with Chipotle Mayo

yield: 8 servings • prep time: 15 minutes, plus 30 minutes to chill
cook time: 20 minutes

**2 large eggs**

**2 tablespoons mayonnaise**

**1 teaspoon hot sauce (see Notes)**

**1 teaspoon Worcestershire sauce**

**1 teaspoon Old Bay seasoning**

**½ teaspoon paprika**

**½ teaspoon ground black pepper**

**¼ teaspoon salt**

**¼ cup chopped red bell peppers**

**2 tablespoons sliced green onions**

**½ cup finely crushed pork rinds**

**¼ cup grated Parmesan cheese**

**1 pound lump crab meat**

**High-quality oil, for frying**

**Chipotle Mayo:**

**½ cup mayonnaise**

**¼ cup sour cream**

**1 chipotle pepper in adobo sauce**

**Pinch of salt**

1. In a medium-size bowl, whisk the eggs. Stir in the mayonnaise, hot sauce, Worcestershire, Old Bay, paprika, black pepper, and salt. Once combined, stir in the red bell peppers and green onions. Gently fold in the pork rinds, Parmesan cheese, and crab meat until well combined.

2. Form the mixture into 8 patties, about 1 inch thick. Place the patties in the refrigerator for 30 minutes.

3. While the crab cakes are chilling, make the chipotle mayo: Put all of the ingredients in a blender or food processor and blend until smooth. Refrigerate until ready to serve.

4. Pour enough oil into a large skillet to evenly coat the bottom of the pan, then set the pan over medium heat. When the oil is hot, gently place 3 or 4 crab cakes in the pan—as many as you can fit without crowding—and fry for 4 to 5 minutes on each side, until golden brown. Repeat with the remaining crab cakes, adding more oil to the pan if needed to prevent sticking. Best if eaten the same day.

*Notes: Crab cakes are often avoided on keto because of the breadcrumbs typically used as a binder. I have taken my low-carb version to the next level by giving you a chipotle mayo to dip them in!*

*A medium-hot hot sauce, such as Frank's RedHot, is ideal for this recipe.*

NET CARBS 1g

| calories | fat | protein | carbs | fiber |
|---|---|---|---|---|
| 234 | 16.4g | 16.4g | 1.3g | 0.4g |

# Bacon Cheeseburger Cauli-Rice Skillet

yield: 6 servings • prep time: 10 minutes • cook time: 30 minutes

**1½ pounds ground beef**

**1 tablespoon dried minced onions**

**1 teaspoon seasoning salt**

**½ cup ketchup (no sugar added)**

**2 tablespoons prepared yellow mustard**

**2 tablespoons Worcestershire sauce**

**1 teaspoon dried dill weed**

**½ teaspoon ground black pepper**

**2 cups cooked cauliflower rice**

**1 cup shredded cheddar cheese**

**6 slices bacon, cooked and crumbled**

**½ cup chopped dill pickles**

**Toasted sesame seeds, for garnish (optional)**

Special Sauce:

**½ cup mayonnaise**

**¼ cup ketchup (no sugar added)**

**1 tablespoon dill pickle relish**

**1 drop liquid stevia**

**Salt and pepper**

1. In a large deep skillet or sauté pan over medium heat, cook the ground beef with the dried minced onions and seasoning salt, crumbling the meat as it cooks, until the beef is cooked through and no longer pink, about 10 minutes. Drain any excess fat.

2. Stir in the ketchup, mustard, Worcestershire, dill, pepper, and cooked cauliflower rice and simmer for 20 minutes to develop the flavors.

3. Meanwhile, make the sauce: In a small bowl, combine the mayonnaise, ketchup, relish, and stevia. Season with salt and pepper to taste.

4. Top the beef mixture with the cheese, bacon, pickles, toasted sesame seeds (if using), and special sauce and serve. Leftovers can be stored in an airtight container in the refrigerator for up to 5 days.

*Notes: This yummy and easy skillet meal is reminiscent of a Big Mac with the "special sauce." The sauce is our favorite!*

*Check the ingredients on your seasoning salt to make sure it doesn't contain sugar. I use Trader Joe's or Redmond Real Salt.*

NET CARBS 5.1g

| calories | fat | protein | carbs | fiber |
|----------|-----|---------|-------|-------|
| 563 | 47.5g | 28.1g | 6.4g | 1.4g |

# Pork Fried Rice

yield: 4 servings • prep time: 10 minutes • cook time: 20 minutes

1 pound bulk breakfast
sausage

2 cloves garlic, minced

¼ cup sliced green onions,
plus more for garnish

¼ cup chopped red bell
peppers

2 tablespoons toasted
sesame oil

1 tablespoon coconut
aminos or gluten-free soy
sauce

2 teaspoons ginger powder

2 cups cooked cauliflower
rice

2 large eggs, whisked

Salt

Sesame seeds, for garnish

1. In a large skillet over medium heat, cook the sausage, crumbling the meat as it cooks, until it is well browned, about 10 minutes. Add the garlic and cook for 1 to 2 more minutes, until fragrant. Add the green onions and red bell peppers and cook until they are tender. Drain any excess fat.

2. In a small bowl, whisk together the sesame oil, aminos, and ginger powder. Pour over the sausage mixture. Add the cauliflower rice to the skillet and continue to cook until the cauli-rice is heated through.

3. Form a well in the center of the skillet. Pour the eggs into the well and let cook without stirring for 3 to 4 minutes, then gently stir until the eggs are soft scrambled. Stir the eggs into the rest of the sausage mixture. Season with salt to taste.

4. Serve garnished with sesame seeds and sliced green onions. Leftovers can be stored in an airtight container in the refrigerator for up to 5 days.

NET CARBS 2.2g

| calories | fat | protein | carbs | fiber |
|----------|-----|---------|-------|-------|
| 394 | 30.9g | 21.6g | 3.2g | 0.9g |

# Brown Sugar-Glazed Meatloaf

yield: 8 servings · prep time: 10 minutes · cook time: 1 hour

**2 pounds ground beef**

**¾ cup finely crushed pork rinds**

**½ cup ketchup (no sugar added)**

**¼ cup brown sugar substitute**

**2 large eggs**

**2 tablespoons chopped fresh parsley, plus more for garnish**

**1 tablespoon Worcestershire sauce**

**1 tablespoon dried minced onions**

**1 teaspoon ginger powder**

**1 teaspoon salt**

**½ teaspoon ground black pepper**

Glaze:

**¼ cup ketchup (no sugar added)**

**2 tablespoons brown sugar substitute**

**Chopped fresh parsley, for garnish (optional)**

1. Preheat the oven to 350°F. Line an 8 by 4-inch loaf pan with parchment paper, allowing some paper to overhang the sides.

2. Put the ground beef in a large mixing bowl and use your hands to break it up. Add the remaining meatloaf ingredients and use your hands to gently combine until all of the ingredients are well incorporated. Be careful not to overwork the meat. Press the meat mixture into the prepared pan.

3. In a small bowl, stir together the glaze ingredients. Spread the glaze evenly over the meatloaf.

4. Bake for 1 hour, or until the juices run clear when the meatloaf is cut. Allow to rest for 10 minutes before slicing. Serve garnished with parsley, if desired. Leftovers can be stored in an airtight container in the refrigerator for up to 5 days.

NET CARBS 2.3g

| calories | fat | protein | carbs | fiber |
|---|---|---|---|---|
| 347 | 24.4g | 24.7g | 2.5g | 0.2g |

# Sheet Pan Smoked Sausage & Peppers

yield: 4 servings · prep time: 15 minutes · cook time: 25 minutes

**1 medium red bell pepper**

**1 medium yellow or orange bell pepper**

**1 medium green bell pepper**

**1 small onion**

**2 tablespoons avocado oil**

**¼ teaspoon salt**

**½ teaspoon ground black pepper**

**10 ounces smoked rope sausage, sliced**

1. Preheat the oven to 400°F. Line a sheet pan with parchment paper.

2. Slice the peppers and onion into strips about ¼ inch thick. Place in a bowl, drizzle with the oil, and sprinkle with the salt and pepper. Toss to coat. Spread the vegetables evenly in the prepared pan.

3. Bake for 15 minutes, then stir and add the sausage to the pan. Cook for 10 more minutes, until the peppers and onions are tender and charred around the edges and the sausage is slightly crispy around the edges. Best if eaten the same day, but leftovers can be stored in an airtight container in the refrigerator for up to 3 days.

*Note: This dish can be served alone or over cauliflower rice.*

NET CARBS 6.8g

| calories | fat | protein | carbs | fiber |
|---|---|---|---|---|
| 306 | 27.3g | 8.6g | 8.8g | 2.1g |

# Corn Dog Casserole

yield: 6 servings · prep time: 15 minutes · cook time: 42 minutes

1 pound ground beef

½ cup chopped onions

2 cloves garlic, minced

4 beef hot dogs, sliced

1 (12-ounce) can tomato paste

½ cup beef broth

1 teaspoon Worcestershire sauce

2 teaspoons chili powder

1 teaspoon ground cumin

1 teaspoon paprika

½ teaspoon salt

**Corn Dog Topping:**

¾ cup finely ground blanched almond flour

1 teaspoon baking powder

⅛ teaspoon salt

1 large egg

2 tablespoons heavy cream

½ cup shredded cheddar cheese

½ teaspoon pure sweet corn extract

1. Preheat the oven to 375°F.

2. In a 12-inch cast-iron skillet or other ovenproof skillet, cook the ground beef with the onions, crumbling the meat as it cooks, until the meat is brown and the onions are tender, about 10 minutes. Add the garlic and cook for 1 to 2 more minutes, until fragrant. Drain any excess fat.

3. Stir in the hot dogs, tomato paste, broth, Worcestershire, chili powder, cumin, paprika, and salt. Lower the heat and simmer for 10 minutes to develop the flavors. Remove the pan from the heat.

4. Meanwhile, make the corn dog topping: In a bowl, whisk together the almond flour, baking powder, and salt. In another bowl, stir together the egg, cream, cheese, and cornbread extract. Fold the wet ingredients into the dry ingredients until combined. The batter will be thick.

5. Drop spoonfuls of the topping mixture evenly over the beef mixture. Place the skillet in the oven and bake for 20 minutes, or until the corn dog topping is cooked through and browned. Leftovers can be stored in an airtight container in the refrigerator for up to 5 days.

NET CARBS 7.8g

| calories | fat | protein | carbs | fiber |
|---|---|---|---|---|
| 461 | 33.7g | 26.6g | 12.6g | 4.9g |

# Roast Beef & Caramelized Onion Pizza

yield: 8 servings • prep time: 20 minutes • cook time: 55 minutes

**Toppings:**

2 tablespoons salted butter

1 medium onion, thinly sliced

½ red bell pepper, thinly sliced

½ cup sliced mushrooms

½ pound thinly sliced deli roast beef, chopped

1 cup shredded mozzarella cheese

**Crust:**

2 cups shredded mozzarella cheese

2 ounces cream cheese (¼ cup)

¾ cup finely ground blanched almond flour

1 large egg

2 teaspoons baking powder

**Sauce:**

1 cup grated Parmesan cheese

½ cup heavy cream

2 tablespoons salted butter

1. Melt the butter in a medium-size skillet over medium heat. Add the onion slices and cook, stirring occasionally, until they start to caramelize, about 15 minutes. Add the bell pepper and mushrooms and continue to cook, stirring occasionally, until the vegetables are tender, about 10 minutes. Add the roast beef and cook for 5 more minutes. Remove the pan from the heat.

2. To make the crust, put the 2 cups of mozzarella and cream cheese in a large microwave-safe bowl. Microwave for 90 seconds, stirring every 30 seconds. Remove from the microwave and stir until melted and smooth.

3. Add the almond flour, egg, and baking powder to the cheese mixture and stir to combine. Microwave for 10 seconds and stir again. Using your hands, mix the ingredients until they're completely combined and a firm dough comes together. If the dough sticks to your hands, put a little olive oil on your hands and continue. Place the dough in the refrigerator for 10 minutes.

4. Preheat the oven to 375°F. Remove the dough from the refrigerator and place it between two sheets of parchment paper. Use a rolling pin to roll the dough to a ¼-inch thickness in your desired shape. Remove the top sheet of the parchment. Lift up and slightly roll the edges of the dough inward to form a crust.

5. Leaving the crust on the bottom sheet of parchment paper, transfer it to a pizza pan, pizza stone, or baking pan. Use a fork to lightly prick holes throughout the crust. Bake the crust for 10 minutes, then remove it from the oven and use a fork to pop any bubbles that have formed. Return the crust to the oven and bake until golden brown, 5 to 8 more minutes. Remove the crust from the oven but leave the oven on. Set the crust aside.

6. To make the sauce, put the Parmesan cheese, cream, and butter in a small saucepan over low heat. Stir continuously until melted and well combined.

NET CARBS 3g

| calories | fat | protein | carbs | fiber |
|---|---|---|---|---|
| 399 | 31.7g | 24.6g | 5.6g | 2.6g |

7. Pour the sauce over the crust and spread evenly. Top evenly with the roast beef mixture and the 1 cup of mozzarella. Bake the pizza for 10 minutes, or until the cheese is melted. Leftovers can be stored in an airtight container in the refrigerator for up to 5 days.

# Buffalo Shrimp & Ranch Cauli-Rice

yield: 4 servings · prep time: 10 minutes (not including time to
make seasoning or dressing) · cook time: 23 minutes

**1 (10-ounce) bag frozen riced cauliflower**

**2 tablespoons salted butter, melted**

**2 tablespoons Ranch Seasoning (page 267)**

**1 pound medium shrimp, peeled and deveined**

**2 tablespoons Buffalo sauce, store-bought or homemade (page 273)**

**½ teaspoon freshly ground black pepper**

**½ cup Ranch Dressing (page 268), for drizzling**

**Dried chives, for garnish**

1. Preheat the oven to 400°F. Line a sheet pan with parchment paper.

2. In a medium-size bowl, mix together the riced cauliflower, melted butter, and ranch seasoning. Spread evenly in the prepared pan. Roast for 15 minutes, or until the cauliflower is tender.

3. Meanwhile, in another medium-size bowl, toss the shrimp with the Buffalo sauce and pepper.

4. Remove the cauliflower rice from the oven and stir. Evenly arrange the shrimp over the cauli-rice. Return the pan to the oven to roast the shrimp until it is pink, 6 to 8 minutes. Watch closely to avoid overcooking the shrimp.

5. Divide among four plates and garnish with a drizzle of ranch dressing and a sprinkle of chives. Serve immediately.

NET CARBS 4.2g

| calories | fat | protein | carbs | fiber |
|----------|-----|---------|-------|-------|
| 256 | 15.3g | 21.3g | 6.1g | 1.9g |

# Cheesy Green Chile Pork Chops

yield: 4 servings • prep time: 10 minutes, plus 30 minutes to marinate

cook time: 22 minutes

**4 bone-in or boneless pork chops, about 1 inch thick**

**Salt and pepper**

Marinade:

**2 tablespoons extra-virgin olive oil**

**½ teaspoon garlic powder**

**½ teaspoon ground cumin**

**½ teaspoon salt**

**½ teaspoon ground black pepper**

Topping:

**1 cup shredded Monterey Jack cheese**

**4 ounces cream cheese (½ cup), softened**

**1 (4-ounce) can diced green chilies**

For Garnish (Optional):

**Extra shredded Monterey Jack cheese**

**Fresh cilantro leaves**

1. Lightly sprinkle the pork chops with salt and pepper on both sides. Place in a large resealable plastic bag.

2. In a small bowl, whisk together the marinade ingredients. Pour the marinade into the bag with the pork chops. Seal the bag and gently toss to coat the chops. Put the bag in the refrigerator to marinate for 30 minutes.

3. Preheat the oven to 350°F. Grease a 9 by 13-inch baking dish.

4. In a small bowl, mix together the topping ingredients.

5. Place the pork chops in the prepared baking dish and evenly spoon the cheese mixture on top of them. Bake for 20 to 22 minutes, until the juices run clear and the internal temperature reaches 145°F. Let the chops rest for 5 minutes before serving.

6. Top the pork chops with additional shredded cheese and fresh cilantro, if desired. Leftovers can be stored in an airtight container in the refrigerator for up to 5 days.

NET CARBS 3.1g

| calories | fat | protein | carbs | fiber |
|---|---|---|---|---|
| 552 | 39.3g | 45.3g | 5g | 1.2g |

# Lasagna-Stuffed Spaghetti Squash

yield: 6 servings · prep time: 15 minutes · cook time: 1 hour 5 minutes

**1 small spaghetti squash (about 3 pounds)**

**2 tablespoons avocado oil**

**Pinch of salt**

**Pinch of ground black pepper**

**1 pound ground beef**

**¼ cup chopped onions**

**2 cloves garlic, minced**

**2 cups marinara sauce, store-bought or homemade (page 271), divided**

**1 cup ricotta cheese**

**1 teaspoon dried basil**

**1 teaspoon ground dried oregano**

**1 teaspoon dried parsley, plus extra for garnish**

**1 cup shredded mozzarella cheese**

1. Preheat the oven to 400°F. Line a sheet pan with parchment paper.

2. Use a knife to pierce holes down both sides of the squash. Microwave the squash for 5 minutes. Carefully remove the squash from the microwave; it will be hot.

3. Cut the squash in half lengthwise. Use a spoon to scoop out the seeds.

4. Drizzle both halves of the squash with the oil and sprinkle evenly with the salt and pepper. Place cut side down in the prepared pan and roast for 35 to 45 minutes, until tender. When done, use a fork to shred the squash, leaving it in the skin. While the squash cooks, prepare the lasagna filling.

5. In a large skillet over medium heat, cook the ground beef with the onions, crumbling the meat as it cooks, until the meat is no longer pink and the onions are tender. Add the garlic and cook for 1 to 2 more minutes, until fragrant. Drain any excess fat.

6. Stir in 1 cup of the marinara and cook until heated through, about 10 minutes, then remove the pan from the heat.

7. In a medium-size bowl, mix together the ricotta, basil, oregano, and parsley until well combined.

8. Layer the top of each spaghetti squash half evenly with half of the meat mixture, half of the ricotta cheese mixture, ½ cup of the remaining marinara, and ½ cup of the mozzarella. Sprinkle some parsley on top.

9. Bake until the cheese melts and starts to bubble around the edges, 10 to 15 minutes. Allow to rest for 10 minutes before serving. Leftovers can be stored in an airtight container in the refrigerator for up to 5 days.

NET CARBS 7.8g

| calories | fat | protein | carbs | fiber |
|---|---|---|---|---|
| 428 | 31.7g | 22.8g | 9.5g | 1.6g |

# Chicken & Dumpling Casserole

yield: 6 servings • prep time: 15 minutes • cook time: 40 minutes

2 tablespoons salted butter

1½ pounds boneless, skinless chicken thighs

½ cup chopped celery

½ cup chopped onions

2 cups chicken broth

½ teaspoon xanthan gum

1 teaspoon chopped fresh parsley, plus more for garnish if desired

½ teaspoon dried basil

½ teaspoon salt

½ teaspoon ground black pepper

**Dumplings:**

1½ cups finely ground blanched almond flour

2 teaspoons baking powder

¼ teaspoon salt

¼ cup heavy cream

2 large eggs

2 tablespoons salted butter, melted (not hot)

1. Melt the butter in a 12-inch skillet over medium heat, then add the chicken, celery, and onions and cook until the vegetables are tender and the chicken is no longer pink in the center, about 10 minutes. Use two forks to shred the chicken in the skillet.

2. Stir the broth into the shredded chicken mixture and sprinkle with the xanthan gum. Add the parsley, basil, salt, and pepper. Lower the heat and simmer until the broth starts to thicken, about 10 minutes. Remove the skillet from the heat.

3. Preheat the oven to 375°F. Grease a 3-quart baking dish.

4. To make the dumpling dough, whisk together the almond flour, baking powder, and salt in a bowl. In another bowl, stir together the cream, eggs, and melted butter. Add the wet ingredients to the dry ingredients and stir until well combined.

5. Spread the chicken mixture in the prepared baking dish. Drop large spoonfuls of the dumpling dough all across the top. Bake for 20 minutes, or until the dumplings are golden brown.

6. Garnish with parsley, if desired. Leftovers can be stored in an airtight container in the refrigerator for up to 5 days.

| | NET CARBS | 4g | | |
|---|---|---|---|---|
| calories | fat | protein | carbs | fiber |
| 417 | 29.6g | 31.7g | 7g | 3.2g |

# Nashville Hot Chicken Tenders

yield: 6 servings · prep time: 15 minutes · cook time: 30 minutes

**High-quality oil, for frying**

**1 large egg**

**½ cup heavy cream**

**1 cup whey protein powder (unflavored and unsweetened)**

**1 teaspoon cayenne pepper**

**½ teaspoon paprika**

**½ teaspoon salt**

**½ teaspoon ground black pepper**

**2 pounds chicken tenderloins**

Spicy Oil:

**½ cup hot cooking oil (from above)**

**1 tablespoon brown sugar substitute**

**1 tablespoon cayenne pepper**

**2 teaspoons paprika**

**½ teaspoon chili powder**

**½ teaspoon garlic powder**

**¼ teaspoon salt**

**½ cup dill pickle chips, for serving**

1. Attach a candy thermometer to a 6-quart Dutch oven or similar-size heavy pot. Pour in 3 inches of oil and set the pot over medium-high heat. Heat the oil to 350°F.

2. While the oil is heating, whisk together the egg and cream in a shallow dish.

3. Put the protein powder and seasonings in a gallon-size resealable plastic bag. Seal and gently shake.

4. Dip both sides of a chicken tenderloin in the egg mixture, allowing the excess to drip back into the bowl, then place it in the bag with the spice mixture. Repeat with 2 or 3 more pieces. Seal the bag and gently shake to coat the chicken. Remove the coated chicken from the bag and set aside. Repeat until all of the chicken tenderloins are coated.

5. Working in small batches, fry the chicken for 3 to 4 minutes, then use tongs to gently turn the tenders and cook for 3 to 4 more minutes, until the chicken is cooked through and golden brown on all sides. Use tongs to transfer the chicken to a wire rack. Repeat with the remaining chicken tenderloins.

6. To make the spicy oil, carefully remove ½ cup of the hot cooking oil from the pot and pour it into a small heatproof bowl. Add the brown sugar substitute, spices, and salt and whisk until the oil and spices are well combined. Brush the spicy oil mixture over the chicken tenders and serve with dill pickle chips. Best if eaten the same day.

*Note: For the spicy oil, you can use more or less cayenne depending on how much heat you prefer. The listed amount is rather spicy, as it should be for this recipe. Nashville hot chicken is hot!*

NET CARBS 0.4g

| calories | fat | protein | carbs | fiber |
|----------|------|---------|-------|-------|
| 281 | 5.1g | 59.6g | 0.4g | 0.1g |

# Meatza

yield: 4 servings • prep time: 10 minutes • cook time: 27 minutes

**Crust:**

**1 pound bulk breakfast sausage**

**1 large egg**

**½ cup grated Parmesan cheese**

**½ teaspoon dried basil**

**½ teaspoon ground dried oregano**

**½ teaspoon dried parsley**

**½ teaspoon garlic powder**

**Suggested Toppings:**

**Marinara sauce, store-bought or homemade (page 271)**

**Cheese(s) of your choice**

**Sliced bell peppers**

**Sliced onions**

**Sliced pepperoni**

**For Garnish (Optional):**

**Chopped fresh basil**

**Red pepper flakes**

1. Preheat the oven to 400°F. Line a sheet pan with parchment paper.

2. Put the sausage in a medium-size bowl and use your hands to break up the meat. Add the rest of the crust ingredients to the bowl and use your hands to incorporate the ingredients into the meat. Turn the meat mixture out into the prepared pan and press it evenly into a ¼-inch-thick crust of your desired shape.

3. Par-bake the crust for 15 minutes, or until the meat is no longer pink. Top with the desired pizza toppings and return to oven for 10 to 12 more minutes, until the toppings are heated through and the cheese is melted.

4. Garnish with fresh basil and/or red pepper flakes, if desired. Leftovers can be stored in an airtight container in the refrigerator for up to 5 days.

*Note: This is a great crust for keeping the carbs in pizza low, and it's sturdy enough to hold all of your favorite toppings!*

| CRUST NET CARBS 0.7g | | | | |
| --- | --- | --- | --- | --- |
| calories | fat | protein | carbs | fiber |
| 345 | 25.2g | 23.2g | 0.8g | 0.2g |

# Slow Cooker Chicken Tacos

yield: about 4 cups shredded chicken, enough for 10 tacos (⅓ heaping cup per serving)

prep time: 15 minutes · cook time: 5 hours

2 tablespoons chili powder

1 tablespoon ground cumin

1 teaspoon paprika

½ teaspoon ground black pepper

½ teaspoon dried oregano leaves

½ teaspoon garlic powder

½ teaspoon onion powder

¾ teaspoon salt

2 pounds boneless, skinless chicken thighs

1 (14.5-ounce) can petite diced tomatoes

1 (4-ounce) can diced green chilies

¼ cup (½ stick) salted butter, sliced

**Keto-friendly taco shells of choice (see Note)**

**Suggested Taco Fixings:**

Shredded lettuce

Sliced avocado

Shredded cheese

Diced tomatoes

Sour cream

Lime wedges

Chopped fresh cilantro

1. Put the spices and salt in a small bowl and mix to combine. Put the chicken in a slow cooker and evenly sprinkle with the spice mix.

2. Spoon the tomatoes and chilies evenly over the chicken. Top with the butter slices. Cover and cook on low until the chicken is fork-tender, 4 to 5 hours. Shred the chicken with two forks.

3. To assemble the tacos, fill keto-friendly taco shells with the shredded chicken and other fixings of your choice. Leftover chicken can be stored in an airtight container in the refrigerator for up to 5 days.

*Note: You can use your choice of keto taco shells. I often use lettuce leaves, low-carb tortillas, or cheese shells. Provolone slices make nice sturdy shells. To make a cheese shell, lay a slice of provolone on a piece of parchment paper. Microwave for 1 minute 30 seconds, until lightly browned and starting to crisp. Some microwaves may take 15 more seconds. Using oven mitts, remove the cheese from the microwave and immediately fold the parchment paper to bend the cheese into a taco shell shape. Keep holding it until it begins to cool and holds its shape. This should only take about 15 seconds.*

CHICKEN NET CARBS 3g

| calories | fat | protein | carbs | fiber |
|---|---|---|---|---|
| 176 | 8.7g | 18.9g | 4.7g | 1.8g |

# Fiesta Casserole

yield: 6 servings • prep time: 10 minutes • cook time: 40 minutes

1½ pounds ground beef

1 clove garlic, minced

1 (8-ounce) package cream cheese, cubed

1 (10-ounce) can diced tomatoes and green chilies

1 tablespoon chili powder

2 teaspoons ground cumin

½ teaspoon salt

½ teaspoon ground black pepper

1 (12-ounce) bag frozen riced cauliflower, cooked following package directions

½ cup shredded Mexican blend cheese

For Garnish/Serving (Optional):

Sliced jalapeño peppers

Sliced green onions

Extra shredded Mexican blend cheese

Sour cream

1. Preheat the oven to 350°F. Grease a 2-quart baking dish.

2. In a large skillet over medium heat, cook the ground beef, crumbling it as it cooks, until browned, about 10 minutes. Add the garlic and cook for 1 to 2 more minutes, until fragrant. Drain any excess fat.

3. Stir in the cream cheese until it is melted. Add the tomatoes and green chilies, chili powder, cumin, salt, pepper, and cooked cauliflower rice. Stir until well combined.

4. Spread the mixture evenly in the prepared baking dish, then sprinkle with the shredded cheese. Bake for 20 to 25 minutes, until the cheese is melted and the casserole starts to bubble around the edges.

5. If desired, garnish with jalapeño and green onion slices, and serve with extra shredded cheese and sour cream. Leftovers can be stored in an airtight container in the refrigerator for up to 5 days.

*Note: This dish is also great served in lettuce wraps or low-carb tortillas.*

NET CARBS 5g

| calories | fat | protein | carbs | fiber |
|----------|-----|---------|-------|-------|
| 463 | 37.2g | 24.4g | 7.7g | 2.8g |

# Shrimp & Andouille Sausage Jambalaya

yield: 6 servings • prep time: 15 minutes • cook time: 50 minutes

**2 tablespoons salted butter**

**½ cup chopped celery**

**½ cup finely chopped onions**

**½ cup chopped green bell peppers**

**2 cloves garlic, minced**

**14 ounces andouille or other smoked sausage, sliced**

**1 (14.5-ounce) can petite diced tomatoes**

**1 cup vegetable broth**

**1 teaspoon paprika**

**½ teaspoon ground dried oregano**

**½ teaspoon salt**

**½ teaspoon ground black pepper**

**¼ teaspoon cayenne pepper**

**¼ teaspoon dried thyme leaves**

**1 bay leaf**

**1 pound medium shrimp, peeled and deveined**

**1 cup cooked cauliflower rice**

For Garnish:

**Sliced green onions**

**Chopped fresh parsley**

1. Melt the butter in a large deep skillet or 6-quart Dutch oven over medium heat. Add the celery, onions, and bell peppers and cook until the vegetables are tender, about 10 minutes. Add the garlic and cook for 1 more minute.

2. Add the sausage to the skillet and cook for 10 minutes, until lightly browned. Stir in the tomatoes, broth, and seasonings. Simmer for 20 minutes to develop the flavors.

3. Add the shrimp and continue cooking until pink, about 5 minutes. Remove the bay leaf. Stir in the cauliflower rice and cook until heated through.

4. Divide the jambalaya among six shallow bowls, garnish with green onions and parsley, and serve. Leftovers can be stored in an airtight container in the refrigerator for up to 5 days.

NET CARBS 4g

| calories | fat | protein | carbs | fiber |
|----------|-----|---------|-------|-------|
| 252 | 16.3g | 20.6g | 5.9g | 1.9g |

# Blackened Salmon

yield: 6 servings • prep time: 5 minutes • cook time: 16 minutes

1 (2½- to 3-pound) salmon
fillet

Salt and pepper

2 tablespoons salted butter,
melted

1 recipe Blackening
Seasoning (page 266)

Lemon wedges, for serving

1. Preheat the oven to 400°F. Line a sheet pan with parchment paper.

2. Use a paper towel to gently pat the salmon fillet dry, then place it in the prepared pan, skin side down. Lightly sprinkle the salmon with salt and pepper. Brush on the melted butter. Evenly sprinkle with the blackening seasoning and use your fingers to gently pat it in.

3. Bake the fish for 12 to 14 minutes, until it flakes with a fork at its thickest part. Turn the oven to broil to brown the top of the salmon. One to two minutes should do it; be careful not to overcook the fish. Serve immediately with lemon wedges. Leftovers can be stored in an airtight container in the refrigerator for up to 3 days.

NET CARBS 2.5g

| calories | fat | protein | carbs | fiber |
|----------|-----|---------|-------|-------|
| 219 | 8.5g | 34.3g | 4.2g | 1.9g |

# Teriyaki Pork Chops

yield: 4 servings · prep time: 10 minutes, plus 2 hours to marinate
(not including time to make sauce) · cook time: 45 minutes

**4 bone-in pork chops, about 1 inch thick**

**Pinch of ground black pepper**

**1 recipe Teriyaki Sauce (page 272)**

For Garnish:

**1 green onion, sliced**

**Toasted sesame seeds**

1. Sprinkle the pork chops with the pepper and place in a resealable plastic bag or a container with a lid. Pour the teriyaki sauce over the chops and seal the bag (or container). Place the chops in the refrigerator to marinate for at least 2 hours.

2. Preheat the oven to 350°F. Grease a baking dish large enough to fit the chops in a single layer.

3. Place the pork chops in the prepared baking dish in a single layer. Pour any remaining teriyaki sauce over the chops. Bake for 45 minutes, or until the internal temperature of the meat reaches 145°F. When done, the juices should run clear.

4. Serve the chops garnished with the green onion and toasted sesame seeds. Leftovers can be stored in an airtight container in the refrigerator for up to 5 days.

Note: *I like to serve these chops with cooked cauliflower rice. They'd also be great with steamed broccoli or mashed cauliflower.*

NET CARBS 2.3g

| calories | fat | protein | carbs | fiber |
|---|---|---|---|---|
| 538 | 32.6g | 51.5g | 2.5g | 0.2g |

# Reuben Wraps

yield: 4 wraps (1 per serving) · prep time: 10 minutes · cook time: 15 minutes

**1 pound deli sliced corned beef**

**1 cup sauerkraut, drained**

**1 cup shredded Swiss cheese**

Dressing:

**½ cup mayonnaise**

**⅓ cup ketchup (no sugar added)**

**¼ cup sour cream**

**2 tablespoons dill pickle relish**

**1 tablespoon prepared horseradish**

**1 teaspoon hot sauce**

**1 teaspoon Worcestershire sauce**

**½ teaspoon onion powder**

**½ teaspoon paprika**

For Serving:

**4 large lettuce leaves, such as green leaf lettuce**

**8 dill pickle chips (optional)**

1. Preheat the oven to 400°F. Line a sheet pan with parchment paper.

2. Divide the corned beef into 4 equal portions. Place them in piles on the sheet pan and top each with ¼ cup of the sauerkraut and ¼ cup of the cheese. Bake for 10 to 15 minutes, until the meat is heated through and the cheese is melted.

3. In a small bowl, mix together the dressing ingredients until well combined.

4. Place each portion of kraut and cheese-topped corned beef in a lettuce leaf and top with a couple of dill pickle chips, if desired. Serve with the dressing.

*Note: I turned my husband's favorite hot sandwich into a lettuce wrap, and it's so good! In addition to the bread, the sauce is a problem when ordering a Reuben at a restaurant; it is normally loaded with sugar. This keto-friendly version is not.*

NET CARBS 4.3g

| calories | fat | protein | carbs | fiber |
|---|---|---|---|---|
| 523 | 35.4g | 37.9g | 4.2g | 0.5g |

# Slow Cooker Cheesesteak Pot Roast

yield: 8 servings · prep time: 20 minutes · cook time: 4 to 6 hours

1 tablespoon avocado oil

1 (3- to 4-pound) beef chuck roast

Salt and pepper

½ cup (1 stick) salted butter, sliced

1 medium onion, sliced

1 cup beef broth

2 tablespoons Worcestershire sauce

2 cloves garlic, minced

1 medium red bell pepper, sliced

1 medium green bell pepper, sliced

Cheese Sauce:

2 tablespoons salted butter

¾ cup heavy cream

1 cup shredded cheddar cheese

½ teaspoon ground mustard

¼ teaspoon salt

1. Heat the oil in a large skillet over medium-high heat. Pat the roast dry and sprinkle both sides with salt and pepper. Sear the roast for 4 to 5 minutes on each side.

2. Transfer the roast to a slow cooker. Place the butter and onion slices evenly over the roast.

3. In a small bowl, combine the broth, Worcestershire, and garlic, then drizzle the mixture over the roast. Cover the slow cooker and cook on low until the roast is tender and starts to easily pull apart with a fork, 3 to 5 hours. Add the red and green bell peppers to the slow cooker and cook for another hour, or until the peppers are tender.

4. When the peppers are nearly done cooking, make the cheese sauce: Heat the butter and cream in a medium-size saucepan over low heat. When the butter is melted and the cream is hot, stir in the cheese, mustard, and salt. Continue to stir until the cheese is melted and the sauce is smooth, about 10 minutes.

5. Use a fork to pull apart the roast into large chunks. Serve topped with the onions and peppers and cheese sauce poured over the top. Leftover pot roast and sauce can be stored in separate airtight containers in the refrigerator for up to 5 days.

NET CARBS 3.4g

| calories | fat | protein | carbs | fiber |
| --- | --- | --- | --- | --- |
| 706 | 54.9g | 48.6g | 4.2g | 0.8g |

*Chapter 6*

## Side Dishes

# Crispy Fried Brussels Sprouts

yield: 4 servings • prep time: 10 minutes • cook time: 15 minutes

**High-quality oil, for frying**

**1 pound Brussels sprouts**

**Kosher-size salt**

**Freshly squeezed lemon juice**

1. Attach a candy thermometer to a 6-quart Dutch oven or similar-size heavy pot. Pour in 3 inches of oil and set the pot over medium-high heat. Heat the oil to 350°F.

2. While the oil is heating, trim the Brussels sprouts and cut them in half.

3. Working in small batches, fry the sprouts until golden brown, 2 to 3 minutes. Sprinkle with salt and lemon juice. Serve immediately. Best if eaten the same day.

*Note: These crispy Brussels sprouts are delicious served with Spicy Ranch Dip (page 98) or with plain ranch dressing (see page 268 for a recipe).*

NET CARBS 2.6g

| calories | fat | protein | carbs | fiber |
|----------|-----|---------|-------|-------|
| 50 | 0g | 3.8g | 7.6g | 5g |

# Smashed Radishes

yield: 4 servings · prep time: 15 minutes · cook time: 40 minutes

**12 ounces radishes, trimmed**

**2 tablespoons extra-virgin olive oil**

**Kosher-size salt**

**½ cup shredded Parmesan cheese**

**Dried parsley, for garnish**

1. Preheat the oven to 400°F. Line a sheet pan with parchment paper.

2. Fill a medium-size pot halfway full of water and bring to a boil over medium-high heat. Add the radishes and cook until tender, 10 to 15 minutes.

3. Drain the radishes in a colander and let them cool for 10 minutes. Put the radishes in the prepared pan. Use the back of a spoon or a potato masher to gently smash each radish, but not until it breaks.

4. Drizzle the radishes with the oil and sprinkle with salt. Top with the cheese and a sprinkle of parsley. Bake for 20 minutes, or until brown around the edges. Turn the oven to broil and cook for 1 to 2 more minutes, until the tops are crispy. Garnish with parsley.

*Note: Smashed potatoes are a popular side dish. Radishes are a great non-starchy potato alternative. I love the crispy, cheesy edges in this dish!*

NET CARBS 3.9g

| calories | fat | protein | carbs | fiber |
|----------|-----|---------|-------|-------|
| 119 | 9.5g | 5.7g | 5.7g | 1.8g |

# Roasted Cheesy Cauli-Mac

yield: 6 servings · prep time: 10 minutes · cook time: 50 minutes

1 large head cauliflower

2 tablespoons avocado oil

1 teaspoon garlic powder

½ teaspoon salt

½ teaspoon ground black pepper

1 cup shredded sharp cheddar cheese

1 cup shredded Monterey Jack cheese

½ cup heavy cream

½ cup grated Parmesan cheese

½ cup finely crushed pork rinds

1. Preheat the oven to 425°F. Line a sheet pan with parchment paper. Grease a 9-inch square baking dish.

2. Cut the head of cauliflower into small florets. Toss with the oil and spread on the prepared sheet pan. Sprinkle evenly with the garlic powder, salt, and pepper. Bake for 25 minutes. Remove the pan from the oven and transfer the roasted cauliflower to a medium-size mixing bowl. Lower the oven temperature to 375°F.

3. In a small saucepan over low heat, combine the cheddar, Monterey Jack, and cream. Stir until melted. Pour the cheese sauce over the cauliflower and gently stir to combine. Transfer the cauliflower mixture to the prepared baking dish.

4. In a small bowl, mix together the Parmesan cheese and pork rinds. Sprinkle evenly over the cauliflower.

5. Bake for 20 to 25 minutes, until bubbling around the edges and browned on top. Allow to rest for 10 minutes before serving. The cheese sauce will thicken as it stands. Leftovers can be stored in an airtight container in the refrigerator for up to 3 days.

*Note: Low-carbers have long used cauliflower as a pasta substitute in mac and cheese recipes. I love the flavor of roasted cauliflower and thought it would work great in a cheesy cauli-mac—and it does!*

NET CARBS 5.6g

| calories | fat | protein | carbs | fiber |
|----------|-----|---------|-------|-------|
| 456 | 34g | 28.7g | 8.4g | 3g |

# Mushroom Cauli-Risotto

yield: 4 servings • prep time: 10 minutes • cook time: 25 minutes

¼ cup (½ stick) salted butter

1 shallot, finely chopped

1 clove garlic, minced

1 cup sliced white mushrooms

1 (10-ounce) bag frozen riced cauliflower

¼ cup dry white wine

¼ cup vegetable broth

½ cup grated Parmesan cheese

¼ cup chopped fresh parsley

Salt and pepper

1. Melt the butter in a large skillet over medium heat. Sauté the shallot and garlic for 5 minutes, then add the mushrooms. Continue cooking and stirring until the mushrooms are tender, 5 to 10 minutes. Remove the mushroom mixture from the skillet and set aside.

2. Add the riced cauliflower to the pan. Cook and stir until tender and cooked through, about 10 minutes.

3. Return the mushroom mixture to the pan. Stir in the wine and broth and continue cooking until the liquids cook down. Stir in the cheese until melted, then stir in the parsley. Season to taste with salt and pepper and serve. Leftovers can be stored in an airtight container in the refrigerator for up to 5 days.

NET CARBS 4.3g

| calories | fat | protein | carbs | fiber |
|----------|-----|---------|-------|-------|
| 185 | 7g | 6.2g | 6.5g | 2.2g |

# Prosciutto Provolone Asparagus

yield: 4 servings • prep time: 10 minutes • cook time: 20 minutes

**1 bunch thin to medium-thick asparagus**

**2 tablespoons avocado oil**

**Salt and pepper**

**6 slices provolone cheese, cut in half**

**12 slices prosciutto**

1. Preheat the oven to 425°F. Line a sheet pan with parchment paper.

2. Break off the tough ends of the asparagus spears. Drizzle the oil over the asparagus and season with a pinch each of salt and pepper.

3. Wrap two or three spears with a piece of provolone and a slice of prosciutto. Arrange the wrapped asparagus in the prepared pan.

4. Roast for 15 to 20 minutes, until the asparagus is tender and the prosciutto starts to crisp. Serve immediately. Leftovers can be stored in an airtight container in the refrigerator for up to 3 days.

NET CARBS 1g

| calories | fat | protein | carbs | fiber |
|----------|-----|---------|-------|-------|
| 307 | 23.3g | 22.4g | 1.1g | 0.1g |

# Asiago Roasted Green Beans

yield: 4 servings • prep time: 10 minutes • cook time: 25 minutes

**1 pound green beans**

**2 tablespoons avocado oil**

**Salt and pepper**

**1 cup shredded Asiago cheese**

1. Preheat the oven to 425°F. Line a sheet pan with parchment paper.

2. Put the green beans in a large bowl. Drizzle with the oil and lightly sprinkle with salt and pepper. Gently toss until the beans are coated in the oil.

3. Spread the green beans evenly in the prepared pan. Roast for 20 minutes, or until the beans are tender, stirring halfway through the cooking time. Remove the green beans from the oven and sprinkle with the cheese. Bake for 5 more minutes, until the cheese is melted. Serve immediately. Leftovers can be stored in an airtight container in the refrigerator for up to 3 days.

NET CARBS 4.9g

| calories | fat | protein | carbs | fiber |
|----------|------|---------|-------|-------|
| 237 | 19.3g | 10.1g | 7.9g | 3.1g |

# Cilantro Lime Cauli-Rice

yield: 4 servings · prep time: 10 minutes · cook time: 15 minutes

2 tablespoons salted butter

1 (12-ounce) bag frozen riced cauliflower

¼ teaspoon garlic powder

Salt and pepper

¼ cup chopped fresh cilantro, plus more for garnish

2 tablespoons freshly squeezed lime juice

Lime wedges, for serving

1. Melt the butter in a medium-size skillet over medium heat. To the skillet, add the riced cauliflower, garlic powder, and a pinch each of salt and pepper. Cook until the cauliflower is tender and cooked through, 12 to 15 minutes.

2. Remove the pan from the heat. Stir in the cilantro and lime juice. Garnish with more cilantro and serve with lime wedges. Leftovers can be stored in an airtight container in the refrigerator for up to 5 days.

NET CARBS 3.2g

| calories | fat | protein | carbs | fiber |
|----------|-------|---------|-------|-------|
| 139 | 12.4g | 3.4g | 5.7g | 2.5g |

# Spaghetti Squash Fritters

yield: 8 fritters (1 per serving) · prep time: 15 minutes,
plus 30 minutes to chill · cook time: 1 hour

1 small spaghetti squash (about 3 pounds)

2 tablespoons avocado oil

Salt and pepper

¾ cup grated Parmesan cheese

1 large egg

2 teaspoons baking powder

1 tablespoon dried chives

½ teaspoon garlic powder

High-quality oil or bacon drippings, for frying

Chopped fresh parsley, for garnish (optional)

1. Preheat the oven to 400°F. Line a sheet pan with parchment paper.

2. Use a knife to pierce holes down both sides of the squash. Microwave the squash for 5 minutes. Carefully remove the squash from the microwave; it will be hot.

3. Cut the squash in half lengthwise. Use a spoon to scoop out the seeds.

4. Drizzle both halves of the squash with the oil and sprinkle evenly with a pinch each of salt and pepper. Place cut side down on the prepared sheet pan and roast for 35 to 45 minutes, until tender. When done, use a fork to shred the squash, then use paper towels or a clean dish towel to squeeze the excess moisture from the squash; this will allow it to hold together better once shaped into fritters.

5. Put the dried squash in a medium-size bowl. Add the Parmesan cheese, egg, baking powder, chives, garlic powder, ½ teaspoon of salt, and ¼ teaspoon of pepper. Mix until well combined.

6. Shape the mixture into 8 fritters about ½ inch thick and place on a sheet pan. Refrigerate the fritters for 30 minutes.

7. Pour enough oil into a large skillet or sauté pan to evenly coat the bottom of the pan, then set the pan over medium heat to heat the oil. Working in batches, gently place the fritters in the hot oil. Fry for 3 to 4 minutes on each side, until golden brown. Serve immediately, garnished with parsley, if desired. Leftovers can be stored in an airtight container in the refrigerator for up to 3 days.

NET CARBS 3.2g

| calories | fat | protein | carbs | fiber |
|---|---|---|---|---|
| 107 | 8g | 5.5g | 4g | 0.8g |

# Southern Summer Squash Casserole

yield: 6 servings • prep time: 10 minutes • cook time: 40 minutes

**2 tablespoons salted butter**

**1 pound yellow squash, cut in half lengthwise and sliced into half-moons**

**½ cup chopped onions**

**2 large eggs**

**¼ cup sour cream**

**½ teaspoon salt**

**¼ teaspoon ground black pepper**

**1 cup shredded cheddar cheese**

**½ cup finely crushed pork rinds**

**¼ cup grated Parmesan cheese**

1. Preheat the oven to 350°F. Grease a 9-inch square baking dish.

2. Melt the butter in a medium-size skillet over medium heat. Cook the squash and onions until the squash is tender and the onions are translucent, about 10 minutes. Remove the skillet from the heat.

3. In a large bowl, whisk the eggs with the sour cream, salt, and pepper. Fold in the squash and cheddar cheese until well combined.

4. Spread the mixture evenly in the prepared baking dish. Bake for 25 minutes, or until browned and bubbly around the edges.

5. Mix together the pork rinds and Parmesan cheese. Sprinkle the topping evenly over the casserole and bake for 5 more minutes, or until the topping is lightly browned.

6. Leftovers can be stored in an airtight container in the refrigerator for up to 2 days.

NET CARBS 3.9g

| calories | fat | protein | carbs | fiber |
|----------|-----|---------|-------|-------|
| 206 | 15g | 11.6g | 5g | 1g |

# Sheet Pan Parmesan Yellow Squash & Zucchini

yield: 6 servings · prep time: 5 minutes · cook time: 25 minutes

**2 medium yellow squash**

**2 medium zucchini**

**2 tablespoons avocado oil**

**Salt and pepper**

**1 cup shredded Parmesan cheese**

1. Preheat the oven to 425°F. Line a sheet pan with parchment paper.

2. Depending on their thickness, halve or quarter the squash and zucchini lengthwise, then slice crosswise into half- or quarter-moons. Toss the squash in the oil and spread evenly in the prepared pan. Lightly sprinkle with salt and pepper.

3. Bake for 20 minutes, or until tender and browning around the edges, stirring halfway through. Remove from the oven and sprinkle evenly with the Parmesan cheese. Return to the oven for 5 more minutes, or until the cheese is melted.

4. For browned and crispy cheese edges, turn the oven to broil and broil for 2 to 3 minutes. Watch closely to avoid burning. Serve immediately. Leftovers can be stored in an airtight container in the refrigerator for up to 3 days.

NET CARBS 3.2g

| calories | fat | protein | carbs | fiber |
|----------|------|---------|-------|-------|
| 121 | 8.5g | 6.5g | 5.2g | 2g |

# Roasted Garlic Chive Cauli-Mash

yield: 6 servings • prep time: 20 minutes • cook time: 45 minutes

**1 whole head garlic**

**1 teaspoon extra-virgin olive oil**

**2 (12-ounce) bags frozen cauliflower florets**

**¼ cup (½ stick) salted butter**

**2 tablespoons sour cream**

**1 tablespoon chopped fresh chives, plus more for garnish**

**Salt and pepper**

1. Preheat the oven to 400°F.

2. Peel off the papery outer layer of the garlic. Use a knife to cut ¼ inch off the top of the garlic head, exposing the individual cloves. Drizzle the exposed cloves with the oil. Wrap the head in aluminum foil to create a pouch, closing it at the top.

3. Place the garlic on a sheet pan and roast for 40 to 45 minutes, until golden and soft.

4. Meanwhile, steam the cauliflower according to the package directions. Make sure the cauliflower is fall-apart tender. Drain the excess liquid.

5. Pull the roasted garlic apart into individual cloves, then gently squeeze the garlic out of each clove.

6. Place the cauliflower and garlic in a food processor or high-powered blender. Add the butter and sour cream. Pulse until the mixture is smooth, then pulse in the chives. Season with salt and pepper to taste. Serve garnished with more chives. Leftovers can be stored in an airtight container in the refrigerator for up to 5 days.

*Note: Roasting garlic caramelizes it slightly and sweetens the flavor a bit. I've used a whole head of roasted garlic here to take ordinary cauli-mash up a notch!*

NET CARBS 4.8g

| calories | fat | protein | carbs | fiber |
|----------|-----|---------|-------|-------|
| 119 | 4.5g | 2.9g | 7.5g | 2.8g |

# Zucchini Carrot Cake

yield: 12 servings • prep time: 25 minutes • cook time: 45 minutes

½ cup brown sugar substitute

½ cup granular sweetener

½ cup coconut oil

4 large eggs

2 teaspoons pure vanilla extract

1½ cups finely ground blanched almond flour

½ cup coconut flour

2 teaspoons baking powder

1 teaspoon ground cinnamon

½ teaspoon xanthan gum

½ teaspoon salt

1 cup shredded zucchini

½ cup shredded carrots

### Cream Cheese Frosting:

1 (8-ounce) package cream cheese, softened

2 tablespoons salted butter, softened

½ cup confectioners' sweetener

½ teaspoon pure vanilla extract

1. Preheat the oven to 350°F. Grease a 12-cup Bundt pan with oil.

2. In a large bowl, whisk together the brown sugar substitute, granular sweetener, oil, eggs, and vanilla until well combined and smooth.

3. In a large bowl, whisk together the flours, baking powder, cinnamon, xanthan gum, and salt. Pour the wet ingredients into the dry ingredients and gently stir until well combined. Fold in the zucchini and carrots.

4. Spoon the batter into the prepared pan, then smooth the top. Bake for 45 minutes, or until a toothpick or tester inserted in the middle of the cake comes out clean. Place the pan on a wire rack to cool completely. Gently loosen the sides of the cooled cake from the pan with a knife and turn the cake onto a cake plate.

5. To make the frosting, put the cream cheese and butter in a large bowl and use a hand mixer to beat the two together until smooth. With the mixer running, add the confectioners' sweetener a little at a time until blended, then add the vanilla. Keep beating until the frosting has an extra light and fluffy texture. Spread the frosting over the top and sides of the cooled cake.

6. Leftover cake can be stored in an airtight container on the counter for up to a day. Thereafter, it should be stored in the refrigerator, where it will keep for up to a week.

NET CARBS 3.6g

| calories | fat | protein | carbs | fiber |
|----------|-----|---------|-------|-------|
| 288 | 26.5g | 6.9g | 6g | 2.7g |

# Salted Dark Chocolate Almond Bark

yield: 8 servings · prep time: 10 minutes, plus 2 hours to chill
cook time: 2 minutes

**1 (4-ounce) bar unsweetened baking chocolate (100% cacao), chopped**

**¼ cup (½ stick) salted butter, softened**

**¼ cup confectioners' sweetener**

**¼ cup sliced almonds, plus more for topping if desired**

**Kosher-size salt, for topping**

1. Line a sheet pan with parchment paper.

2. In a small microwave-safe bowl, microwave the chocolate until melted, stirring every 20 seconds. Stir in the butter until it melts.

3. Stir in the sweetener and mix until completely dissolved. Fold in the almonds until well combined.

4. Spread the mixture evenly in the prepared pan. Sprinkle with salt and, if desired, some additional almonds. Place in the refrigerator until firm, about 2 hours. Break into pieces and serve. Leftovers can be stored in an airtight container in refrigerator for up to a week.

NET CARBS 1.4g

| calories | fat | protein | carbs | fiber |
|----------|------|---------|-------|-------|
| 123 | 7.9g | 2g | 3.1g | 1.7g |

# Lemon Cheesecake Mousse

yield: 4 servings · prep time: 10 minutes, plus 2 hours to chill

1 (8-ounce) package cream cheese, softened

½ cup confectioners' sweetener

Grated zest and juice of 1 lemon

1 cup heavy cream

½ teaspoon pure vanilla extract

Raspberries, for garnish (optional)

1. In a medium-size mixing bowl, beat the cream cheese and sweetener with a hand mixer until fluffy. Add the lemon zest and juice and mix for 1 minute.

2. Pour the cream and vanilla into a large mixing bowl and whip with the hand mixer until stiff peaks form. Fold in the cream cheese mixture until well combined. Cover and refrigerate for at least 2 hours before serving.

3. Garnish each serving with a few raspberries, if desired. Leftover mousse can be stored in an airtight container in the refrigerator for up to 3 days.

NET CARBS 1.9g

| calories | fat | protein | carbs | fiber |
|----------|-----|---------|-------|-------|
| 246 | 21.5g | 8.3g | 2.3g | 0.4g |

# Loaded N'oatmeal Cookies

yield: 18 cookies (1 per serving) · prep time: 10 minutes
cook time: 25 minutes

**1½ cups finely ground blanched almond flour**

**1 teaspoon baking powder**

**1 teaspoon baking soda**

**¼ teaspoon salt**

**½ cup (1 stick) salted butter, softened**

**¼ cup granulated sweetener**

**¼ cup brown sugar substitute**

**1 large egg**

**1 teaspoon pure vanilla extract**

**⅓ cup unsweetened shredded coconut**

**⅓ cup chopped raw walnuts**

**¼ cup hemp hearts**

**¼ cup sugar-free chocolate chips**

**¼ cup sugar-free white chocolate chips**

**Kosher-size salt, for topping (optional)**

1. Place an oven rack in the middle of the oven. Preheat the oven to 350°F. Line two baking sheets with parchment paper.

2. In a medium-size bowl, whisk together the almond flour, baking powder, baking soda, and salt.

3. In a separate medium-size bowl, use a hand mixer on medium speed to beat the butter, granulated sweetener, and brown sugar substitute until smooth and creamy. On low speed, gradually mix in the egg and vanilla until combined. Mix in the flour mixture a little at a time until combined. Stir in the coconut, walnuts, hemp hearts, and chocolate chips.

4. Using a medium-size ice cream scoop, scoop nine 2-inch balls of dough onto each prepared baking sheet, spaced 2 inches apart. (If you don't have an ice cream scoop, use your hands to form the dough into balls.) Bake the cookies one pan at a time for 10 to 12 minutes, until the cookies are golden brown and set around the edges. They will still be slightly soft in the center.

5. Sprinkle the hot cookies with kosher-size salt, if desired. Allow them to cool for 10 minutes, then use a spatula to gently transfer them to a wire rack to cool completely. Leftovers can be stored in an airtight container on the counter for up to a week.

NET CARBS 3.3g

| calories | fat | protein | carbs | fiber |
|----------|-----|---------|-------|-------|
| 165 | 15.2g | 4.1g | 6.1g | 2.8g |

# Edible Cookie Dough

yield: 2 servings • prep time: 5 minutes, plus 1 hour to chill

¼ cup (½ stick) salted butter, softened

¼ cup confectioners' sweetener

⅛ teaspoon salt

¼ teaspoon pure vanilla extract

½ cup finely ground blanched almond flour

1 tablespoon heavy cream

¼ cup sugar-free chocolate chips

In a small bowl, use a spoon to mix together the butter, sweetener, salt, and vanilla until well combined. Add the almond flour and cream and stir well until combined. Stir in the chocolate chips. Place the bowl in the refrigerator for at least 1 hour before serving. The cookie dough can be stored in an airtight container in the refrigerator for up to 5 days.

> *Note: This creation stemmed from my love of eating cookie dough straight from the fridge! No worries, there are no eggs in this version. It would be great on top of other desserts or in keto ice cream.*

NET CARBS 3.5g

| calories | fat | protein | carbs | fiber |
|----------|-----|---------|-------|-------|
| 499 | 49.2g | 6.2g | 14.1g | 10.6g |

# No-Bake Strawberry Cream Pie

yield: 8 servings • prep time: 10 minutes (not including time
to make crust), plus 2 hours to chill

**1 (8-ounce) package cream cheese, softened**

**½ cup granular sweetener**

**½ cup heavy cream**

**1 teaspoon pure vanilla extract**

**1 cup chopped strawberries**

**1 prebaked Graham Cracker Crust (page 276)**

1. In a medium-size mixing bowl, use a hand mixer to beat the cream cheese, sweetener, and cream until smooth and creamy. Stir in the vanilla. Gently fold in the strawberries.

2. Pour the mixture into the prepared pie crust. Place in the refrigerator to chill for at least 2 hours before serving. Leftover pie can be stored, covered, in the refrigerator for up to 3 days.

NET CARBS 4.2g

| calories | fat | protein | carbs | fiber |
|----------|-----|---------|-------|-------|
| 322 | 30.6g | 6.5g | 6.8g | 2.6g |

# German Chocolate Cake

yield: 8 servings • prep time: 25 minutes, plus 30 minutes to rest
cook time: 50 minutes

## Cake:

¾ cup finely ground blanched almond flour

2 tablespoons coconut flour

½ cup cocoa powder

1 tablespoon instant espresso powder

2 teaspoons baking powder

½ teaspoon xanthan gum

¼ teaspoon salt

¼ cup (½ stick) salted butter, softened

½ cup granular sweetener

3 large eggs

½ cup unsweetened almond milk

1 teaspoon white vinegar

½ teaspoon pure vanilla extract

## Frosting:

¾ cup heavy cream

2 large egg yolks

¼ cup (½ stick) salted butter

½ cup brown sugar substitute

¼ teaspoon salt

½ cup chopped roasted pecans

½ cup unsweetened coconut flakes

½ teaspoon pure vanilla extract

⅓ cup roasted pecan halves, for garnish

## To make the cake:

1. Preheat the oven to 350°F. Grease a 9-inch round cake pan.

2. In a medium-size mixing bowl, whisk together the flours, cocoa powder, espresso powder, baking powder, xanthan gum, and salt. In a large mixing bowl, use a hand mixer to beat the butter and granular sweetener until smooth. Mix in the eggs one at a time. Add the almond milk, vinegar, and vanilla and mix again. With the mixer on low speed, blend in the flour mixture a little at a time.

3. Pour the batter into the prepared pan, then smooth the top. Bake for 35 to 45 minutes, until a toothpick or tester inserted into the middle of the cake comes out clean. Place the pan on a wire rack and allow the cake to cool. Gently loosen the sides of the cake from the pan with a knife and turn it onto a cake plate.

## To make the frosting and assemble the cake:

4. In a medium-size saucepan, combine the cream, egg yolks, butter, brown sugar substitute, and salt. Cook over low heat, stirring continuously, until the frosting thickens, about 5 minutes. Stir in the chopped pecans, coconut flakes, and vanilla. Let the frosting cool for 15 minutes, then pour it over the top of the cake and spread it evenly. Garnish with the pecan halves.

5. Let the cake rest for at least 30 minutes before serving. Leftover cake can be stored, covered, on the counter for up to a day or stored in an airtight container in the refrigerator for up to a week.

NET CARBS 4.1g

| calories | fat | protein | carbs | fiber |
|----------|-----|---------|-------|-------|
| 350 | 33g | 7.7g | 7.8g | 3.7g |

# Muddy Buddies

yield: 6 servings • prep time: 10 minutes • cook time: 2 minutes

1 (6-ounce) bag pork rinds

½ cup sugar-free chocolate chips

¼ cup smooth natural peanut butter

3 tablespoons salted butter

½ teaspoon pure vanilla extract

1 drop liquid stevia

¼ cup confectioners' sweetener

1. Break the pork rinds into bite-size pieces and place them in a bowl with a lid.

2. In a small microwave-safe bowl, microwave the chocolate and peanut butter until completely melted, stirring every 20 seconds. Add the butter and stir until melted and well combined. Stir in the vanilla and stevia.

3. Pour the chocolate mixture over the pork rinds and gently stir until the pork rinds are completely coated. Add the confectioners' sweetener. Put the lid on the bowl and shake until completely coated. Leftovers can be stored in an airtight container in the refrigerator for up to a week.

*Note: I enjoy making candies and desserts at Christmastime. This recipe, which uses pork rinds, is a delicious alternative to the high-sugar version of muddy buddies that I used to make using cereal.*

NET CARBS 3.3g

| calories | fat | protein | carbs | fiber |
|----------|------|---------|-------|-------|
| 289 | 14.2g | 24.3g | 9.1g | 5.9g |

# Peanut Butter Pie with Chocolate Crust

## Chocolate Crust:

**1½ cups finely ground blanched almond flour**

**½ cup cocoa powder**

**½ cup confectioners' sweetener**

**2 teaspoons instant espresso powder**

**⅛ teaspoon salt**

**½ cup (1 stick) salted butter, melted**

## Filling:

**1 (8-ounce) package cream cheese, softened**

**½ cup granular sweetener**

**¾ cup smooth natural peanut butter**

**1 cup heavy cream**

**1 teaspoon pure vanilla extract**

## For Garnish (Optional):

**Sugar-free chocolate syrup**

**Whipped cream**

1. Preheat the oven to 350°F. Grease a 9-inch pie plate with oil.

2. To make the crust, whisk together the almond flour, cocoa powder, confectioners' sweetener, espresso powder, and salt in a medium-size mixing bowl. Stir in the melted butter until well mixed. Press the dough evenly across the bottom and up the sides of the prepared pie plate. Use a fork to lightly prick the bottom of the crust several times. Bake the crust for 10 to 12 minutes, until firm. Set aside to cool completely.

3. To make the filling, put the cream cheese and granular sweetener in a large mixing bowl. Use a hand mixer on medium speed to beat until fluffy. With the mixer still on medium speed, mix in the peanut butter until smooth.

4. Pour the cream and vanilla into a medium-size mixing bowl. Use the mixer on medium speed to whip until stiff peaks form. Fold the whipped cream into the peanut butter mixture until completely combined.

5. Pour the filling into the crust and use a spatula to smooth the top. Garnish with chocolate syrup and whipped cream, if desired. Chill the pie in the refrigerator for at least 2 hours before serving. Leftover pie can be stored, covered, in the refrigerator for up to a week.

*Note: When I need a keto-friendly chocolate syrup for recipes like this one, I use Choczero chocolate syrup.*

NET CARBS 6.5g

| calories | fat | protein | carbs | fiber |
|----------|-----|---------|-------|-------|
| 514 | 47.6g | 12.6g | 11.6g | 5.1g |

# Skillet Blondie for Two

option

yield: 2 servings · prep time: 5 minutes · cook time: 18 minutes

½ cup natural almond butter

1 large egg

¼ cup brown sugar substitute

½ teaspoon baking powder

¼ teaspoon pure vanilla extract

¼ cup sugar-free chocolate chips

Whipped cream, for serving (optional)

1. Preheat the oven to 350°F. Grease a 6-inch cast-iron skillet or cake pan.

2. In a small bowl, use a spoon to mix the almond butter, egg, brown sugar substitute, baking powder, and vanilla until well combined. Stir in the chocolate chips.

3. Evenly spread the dough in the skillet. Bake for 16 to 18 minutes, until the center is set. Allow to cool completely before cutting, or serve warm with a dollop of whipped cream.

NET CARBS 6.1g

| calories | fat | protein | carbs | fiber |
|----------|------|---------|-------|-------|
| 590 | 42.5g | 16.6g | 24.6g | 18.4g |

# Peanut Butter Cup Bars

yield: 16 bars (1 per serving) • prep time: 10 minutes, plus 1 hour 10 minutes to freeze

cook time: 4 minutes

**1 cup natural peanut butter**

**½ cup (1 stick) salted butter**

**¾ cup confectioners' sweetener**

**1 teaspoon pure vanilla extract**

**½ cup sugar-free chocolate chips, or 4 ounces sugar-free chocolate, chopped**

1. Line an 8-inch square baking pan with parchment paper.

2. Place the peanut butter and butter in a medium-size microwave-safe bowl. Microwave, stirring every 30 seconds, until completely melted.

3. Add the sweetener and vanilla. Stir until smooth, then pour the mixture into the prepared pan. Place the pan in the freezer for 10 minutes.

4. Put the chocolate chips in a small microwave-safe bowl. Microwave until melted, stirring every 20 seconds.

5. Remove the pan from the freezer. Pour the melted chocolate over the peanut butter layer and use the back of a spoon or a spatula to evenly spread the chocolate to the edges of the pan. Return the pan to the freezer for 1 hour.

6. Remove the pan from the freezer and let sit on the counter for 10 minutes before cutting into bars with a sharp knife. Leftovers can be stored in an airtight container in the refrigerator for up to 2 weeks.

*Note: This recipe has been a favorite among my blog readers for years, so I had to include it here for the rest of my Southern Keto fans. To me, it tastes exactly like Reese's Peanut Butter Cups! You can use any kind of keto-friendly chocolate you enjoy.*

NET CARBS 2.4g

| calories | fat | protein | carbs | fiber |
|----------|------|---------|-------|-------|
| 134 | 9.1g | 7.6g | 6.3g | 4g |

# Lisa's Peanut Butter Cheesecake Brownies

yield: 18 brownies (1 per serving) · prep time: 15 minutes · cook time: 37 minutes

**Brownie Layer:**

1 (4-ounce) bar unsweetened baking chocolate (100% cacao), chopped

¾ cup (1½ sticks) salted butter

¾ cup brown sugar substitute

¾ cup granular sweetener

4 large eggs

1¼ cups finely ground blanched almond flour

**Peanut Butter Cheesecake Layer:**

1 (8-ounce) package cream cheese, softened

½ cup natural peanut butter

1 large egg

½ cup granular sweetener

1. Preheat the oven to 350°F. Grease a 9 by 13-inch baking pan or line it with parchment paper.

2. To make the brownie layer, put the chocolate and butter in a large microwave-safe bowl. Microwave, stirring every 30 seconds, until melted, then stir until very well combined. Add the sweeteners and stir until dissolved and smooth. Add the eggs one at a time, stirring after each addition. Add the almond flour a little bit at a time, stirring after each addition, until well combined. Spread the batter evenly in the prepared pan.

3. To make the cheesecake layer, put the cream cheese and peanut butter in a medium-size mixing bowl. Use a hand mixer to beat them together, then add the egg and sweetener and beat until smooth. Evenly drop the cheesecake mixture by the spoonful over the brownie batter. Use a knife to cut through the batter and swirl it back and forth a few times to create a marbled effect.

4. Bake for 30 to 35 minutes, until the brownies are set and a toothpick or tester inserted in the middle comes out clean. Allow to cool completely before cutting and serving. Leftovers can be stored, covered, on the counter for up to a day; thereafter, store them in an airtight container in the refrigerator for up to a week.

*Note: My friend Lisa and I often enjoy keto meals together. We both love all things peanut butter and chocolate. Last summer she created this dessert, and it quickly became a favorite of ours.*

NET CARBS 2.7g

| calories | fat | protein | carbs | fiber |
|----------|-----|---------|-------|-------|
| 231 | 21g | 8.1g | 5.2g | 2.8g |

# Toasted Coconut Bars

yield: 10 bars (1 per serving) · prep time: 15 minutes, plus 1 hour to chill

cook time: 8 minutes

**1½ cups unsweetened shredded coconut**

**1 (3.5-ounce) bar ultra-dark chocolate (90% cacao), chopped**

**¼ cup (½ stick) salted butter**

**½ cup confectioners' sweetener**

**¼ cup coconut oil (see Note)**

**2 tablespoons heavy cream**

1. Preheat the oven to 325°F. Line a sheet pan with parchment paper.

2. Spread the coconut in a thin layer in the prepared pan. Bake for 5 minutes, then stir the coconut. Return the pan to the oven and continue to bake just until golden brown. Coconut can burn quickly, so keep a close eye on it. Remove the coconut from the pan and allow to cool.

3. Line the bottom and sides of a 9 by 5-inch loaf pan with parchment paper. Place the chocolate and butter in a medium-size microwave-safe bowl. Microwave, stirring every 30 seconds, until completely melted.

4. Put the sweetener, coconut oil, and cream in a medium-size bowl and stir until smooth. Fold in the toasted coconut until well combined. Spread the mixture into a thin, even layer in the prepared loaf pan.

5. Pour the melted chocolate mixture over the coconut layer and smooth the top. Cover and refrigerate until firm, at least 1 hour. Cut into bars and serve. Leftovers can be stored in an airtight container in the refrigerator for up to a week.

*Note: If your coconut oil isn't liquid in the jar, melt it before using it in this recipe. You can also buy coconut oil that remains liquid even in cool temperatures.*

| | NET CARBS 2.7g | | | |
|---|---|---|---|---|
| calories | fat | protein | carbs | fiber |
| 188 | 14.4g | 3.8g | 5.9g | 3.3g |

# Chocolate Cookie Crumbs

yield: 8 servings (¼ cup per serving) · prep time: 5 minutes · cook time: 15 minutes

**1½ cups finely ground blanched almond flour**

**¾ cup granular sweetener**

**½ cup (1 stick) salted butter, melted**

**½ cup Dutch-process cocoa powder**

**⅛ teaspoon salt**

1. Preheat the oven to 350°F. Line a sheet pan with parchment paper.

2. Put all of the ingredients in a large bowl. Stir until well combined.

3. Spread the mixture evenly in the prepared pan. Bake for 15 minutes, stirring halfway through. The cookie crumbs will still be soft and look wet. Allow them to completely cool in the pan, then stir to break them up more. Store in an airtight container on the counter for up to a week.

*Notes: This recipe requires Dutch-process, or "Dutched," cocoa powder to replicate the dark color and taste of chocolate sandwich cookies. It's what gives these cookie crumbs their distinct chocolate sandwich cookie flavor.*

*These cookie crumbs are delicious enjoyed on their own, as a snack, or used for desserts and toppings, such as ice cream, pies, and smoothies. In this book, they're featured in the Dirt Cake (page 242).*

NET CARBS 2.7g

| calories | fat | protein | carbs | fiber |
|----------|------|---------|-------|-------|
| 242 | 22.4g | 5.1g | 6.5g | 3.9g |

# Dirt Cake

yield: 8 servings • prep time: 30 minutes, plus 8 hours to chill

**Chocolate Mousse:**

2 teaspoons grass-fed gelatin powder

¼ cup cold water

2 tablespoons very hot water

1½ cups heavy cream

½ cup granular sweetener

½ cup cocoa powder

**Whipped Cream:**

1 cup heavy cream

2 tablespoons granular sweetener

1 teaspoon pure vanilla extract

1 recipe Chocolate Cookie Crumbs (page 240), divided

**To make the mousse:**

1. In a small bowl, sprinkle the gelatin over the cold water. Let stand for 1 minute to soften. Add the hot water, stirring until the gelatin is completely dissolved.

2. In a medium-size mixing bowl, use a hand mixer on medium speed to whip the cream with the sweetener until soft peaks form. Scrape down the sides of the bowl, lower the speed, and slowly add the cocoa powder while mixing. Increase the speed to medium and continue mixing until the mixture is stiff. Pour in the gelatin mixture and beat until well blended.

**To make the whipped cream:**

In a medium-size mixing bowl, use a hand mixer to whip the cream with the sweetener and vanilla until stiff peaks form.

**To layer the trifle:**

Sprinkle one-third of the cookie crumbs across the bottom of an 8-inch-diameter trifle bowl or a large glass bowl or container. Spread half of the mousse over the cookie crumbs, followed by half of the whipped cream. Sprinkle another third of the cookie crumbs on top, then follow with the rest of the mousse and whipped cream. Top with the rest of the cookie crumbs. Cover and refrigerate for at least 8 hours or overnight before serving. Leftovers can be stored, covered, in the refrigerator for up to 5 days.

NET CARBS 3.8g

| calories | fat | protein | carbs | fiber |
|---|---|---|---|---|
| 508 | 48.1g | 9.4g | 9.6g | 5.9g |

# Magic Layer Bars

yield: 12 bars (1 per serving) · prep time: 10 minutes (not including time to make sweetened condensed milk), plus 1 hour to chill · cook time: 30 minutes

¼ cup (½ stick) salted butter, melted

1¼ cups finely ground blanched almond flour

2 tablespoons granular sweetener

1 teaspoon pure vanilla extract

1 cup unsweetened shredded coconut

¾ cup sugar-free chocolate chips

1 cup Sweetened Condensed Milk (page 275), cooled

½ cup chopped raw pecans

1. Preheat the oven to 350°F. Grease a 9-inch square baking pan or line it with parchment paper.

2. In a small bowl, stir together the melted butter, almond flour, sweetener, and vanilla. Press the mixture evenly into the bottom of the prepared pan.

3. Layer the rest of the ingredients in the pan in this order: coconut, chocolate chips, sweetened condensed milk, and pecans.

4. Bake for 25 to 30 minutes, until the edges of the bars turn golden brown and start to pull away from the sides of the pan.

5. Remove from the oven and allow to cool completely. Cover and refrigerate for at least 1 hour to allow the bars to firm up before cutting and serving. Leftovers can be stored at room temperature, but it is better to store them in an airtight container in the refrigerator for up to 5 days.

> *Note: To make these bars come together quickly, prepare the sweetened condensed milk the day before.*

NET CARBS 3.2g

| calories | fat | protein | carbs | fiber |
|----------|------|---------|-------|-------|
| 277 | 22.5g | 5.4g | 8.6g | 5.4g |

# Banana Cream Pie

yield: 8 servings • prep time: 10 minutes (not including time to make crust), plus 6 hours to chill

**1 (8-ounce) package cream cheese, softened**

**½ cup confectioners' sweetener**

**1 cup heavy cream**

**2 teaspoons pure banana extract**

**1 prebaked Graham Cracker Crust (page 276)**

1. In a medium-size mixing bowl, use a hand mixer to beat the cream cheese with the sweetener until well combined. Scrape down the sides of the bowl. Lower the speed of the mixer and blend in the cream. Continue beating until the mixture is light and fluffy. Blend in the banana extract.

2. Pour the cream cheese mixture into the prebaked crust. Use the back of a spoon or a spatula to smooth the top. Cover the pie and refrigerate for 6 hours to overnight before serving. The longer the pie chills, the more the banana flavor will develop. Leftover pie can be stored, covered, in the refrigerator for up to 5 days.

*Note: For a more authentic look, you can add a few drops of yellow food coloring to the banana cream filling.*

NET CARBS 3.5g

| calories | fat | protein | carbs | fiber |
|----------|-----|---------|-------|-------|
| 367 | 35.5g | 6.9g | 5.7g | 2.2g |

# Toasted Coconut Custard

yield: 8 servings · prep time: 5 minutes, plus 6 hours to chill · cook time: 20 minutes

**Toasted Coconut:**

½ cup unsweetened
shredded coconut

**Custard:**

1 (13.5-ounce) can full-fat
coconut milk

½ cup heavy cream

½ cup granular sweetener

4 large egg yolks, whisked

½ teaspoon xanthan gum

1 teaspoon pure vanilla
extract

Whipped cream, for serving
(optional)

**To make the toasted coconut:**

1. Preheat the oven to 325°F. Line a sheet pan with parchment paper.

2. Spread the coconut in a thin layer in the prepared pan. Bake for 5 minutes, stir the coconut, then return to the oven and bake until golden brown. It shouldn't take more than another 2 to 3 minutes. Keep a close eye on it, as coconut can burn quickly. Remove the toasted coconut from the pan and allow to cool.

**To make the custard:**

1. In a medium-size saucepan over medium heat, whisk together the coconut milk, cream, and sweetener. Bring to a boil, whisking occasionally. Boil for 2 minutes, then reduce the heat to medium-low.

2. Remove ½ cup of the mixture and slowly pour it into the whisked egg yolks while whisking briskly so the eggs don't scramble. Slowly pour the egg yolk mixture back into the pan. Evenly sprinkle the xanthan gum over the custard mixture, continuing to whisk. Continue to cook, whisking often, until the custard starts to thicken and coats the back of a spoon, about 10 minutes.

3. Remove the pan from the heat and stir in the vanilla. Allow to cool. The custard will continue to thicken as it cools.

4. Pour the custard into a serving bowl. Sprinkle the toasted coconut over the custard. Cover and refrigerate for 6 hours to overnight. The custard will thicken more as it's refrigerated.

5. Serve topped with whipped cream, if desired. Leftovers can be stored, covered, in the refrigerator for up to 5 days.

NET CARBS 2g

| calories | fat | protein | carbs | fiber |
|----------|-----|---------|-------|-------|
| 189 | 18g | 3.8g | 2.9g | 0.9g |

# Red Velvet Cake

yield: 12 servings · prep time: 45 minutes, plus 30 minutes to chill if desired
cook time: 30 minutes

## Cake:

**2 cups finely ground blanched almond flour**

**½ cup coconut flour**

**¼ cup cocoa powder**

**1 teaspoon baking powder**

**1 teaspoon baking soda**

**½ teaspoon salt**

**½ cup heavy cream**

**½ cup water**

**1 tablespoon white vinegar**

**½ cup (1 stick) salted butter, softened**

**¾ cup granular sweetener**

**4 large eggs, room temperature**

**1 cup sour cream**

**2 teaspoons pure vanilla extract**

**1 (1-ounce) bottle red food coloring**

## Frosting:

**12 ounces cream cheese (1½ cups), softened**

**½ cup (1 stick) salted butter, softened**

**1 cup confectioners' sweetener**

**1 teaspoon pure vanilla extract**

## To make the cake:

1. Preheat the oven to 350°F. Grease two 9-inch round cake pans or line them with parchment paper cut to fit, then grease the sides.

2. In a medium-size bowl, whisk together the flours, cocoa powder, baking powder, baking soda, and salt.

3. To make a buttermilk alternative, put the cream, water, and vinegar in a small glass bowl or 1-cup liquid measuring cup. Stir and set aside to sour.

4. Using a hand mixer and a large bowl, or a stand mixer fitted with the flat beater attachment, cream the butter and sweetener on medium speed for 4 to 5 minutes, until fluffy. Beat in the eggs one at a time, scraping down the sides of the bowl after each addition. Beat in the sour cream and vanilla.

5. With the mixer on low speed, add the dry ingredients a little at a time, alternating with the buttermilk alternative. Scrape down the sides. Beat in the food coloring until the color is even. The batter will be thick.

6. Divide the cake batter evenly between the prepared pans. Smooth the tops.

7. Bake for 30 minutes, or until a toothpick or tester inserted into the center of the cakes comes out clean. Place the pans on a wire rack to cool completely.

## To make the frosting:

Using a hand mixer and a large bowl, or a stand mixer fitted with the whisk attachment, beat the cream cheese and butter together on high speed until smooth. Scrape down the sides of the bowl. Beat in the sweetener on low speed a little at a time. Scrape down the sides. Beat in the vanilla until combined, then increase the speed to high and beat for 2 to 3 for minutes, until light and fluffy.

NET CARBS 5.1g

| calories | fat | protein | carbs | fiber |
|---|---|---|---|---|
| 455 | 43.7g | 9.5g | 8.3g | 3.2g |

**To assemble the cake:**

Carefully unpan the cakes and place one cake layer on a cake stand or plate. Use an offset spatula to spread the top with frosting. Carefully top with the second cake layer and spread the rest of the frosting across the top and down the sides. For cleaner slices, place the cake in the refrigerator for 30 minutes before slicing and serving. Leftovers can be stored in an airtight container in the refrigerator for up to 5 days.

# Forgotten Cookies

yield: 24 cookies (2 per serving) · prep time: 10 minutes, plus overnight to rest
cook time: 10 minutes

**2 large egg whites, room temperature**

**½ cup confectioners' sweetener**

**⅛ teaspoon salt**

**1 teaspoon pure vanilla extract**

**½ cup chopped raw pecans**

**½ cup sugar-free chocolate chips**

1. Preheat the oven to 350°F. Line a sheet pan with parchment paper.

2. In a medium-size mixing bowl, beat the egg whites with a hand mixer until foamy. While beating, slowly add the sweetener, salt, and vanilla to the egg whites. Continue to beat until stiff peaks form.

3. Use a spatula to gently fold in the pecans and chocolate chips, being careful not to break down the egg whites.

4. Drop teaspoonfuls of the meringue onto the prepared baking sheet. Bake the cookies for 10 minutes, then turn the oven off. To keep the heat in, do not open the oven door.

5. Leave the cookies in the oven overnight, or for 8 to 10 hours. The cookies are best if eaten the same day but can be stored covered at room temperature for up to 3 days.

*Note: This is an old recipe for delicious little meringue cookies. The name comes from the baking process: you place them in a preheated oven, turn off the heat, and forget about them!*

NET CARBS 1.5g

| calories | fat | protein | carbs | fiber |
|----------|-----|---------|-------|-------|
| 43 | 3.1g | 1.3g | 3.8g | 2.3g |

# Strawberry-Infused Lemonade

yield: six 8-ounce servings · prep time: 10 minutes, plus 2 hours to chill

**7 lemons, divided**

**2 cups hot water**

**¾ cup granular sweetener**

**4 cups water**

**1 cup sliced strawberries**

1. Firmly roll six of the lemons on a cutting board, then cut them in half and juice them. Slice the remaining lemon.

2. Pour the hot water into a 2-quart pitcher, then add the sweetener and stir until it is dissolved. Add the 4 cups of water, strawberries, lemon juice, and lemon slices and stir.

3. Cover and refrigerate for at least 2 hours before serving. Leftover lemonade can be stored, covered, in the refrigerator for up to 3 days.

NET CARBS 4g

| calories | fat | protein | carbs | fiber |
|----------|------|---------|-------|-------|
| 16 | 0.2g | 0.3g | 4.5g | 0.5g |

# Frosé

yield: four 9-ounce servings • prep time: 10 minutes, plus 4 hours to freeze

**1 (750-ml) bottle dry rosé wine**

**¼ cup vodka**

**1½ cups strawberries, hulled, plus 4 more for garnish if desired**

**2 tablespoons granular sweetener**

**2 tablespoons freshly squeezed lemon juice**

1. Place all of the ingredients in a blender and blend until smooth, with no lumps.

2. Pour the mixture into a 9 by 13-inch baking pan and place in the freezer. Freeze for at least 4 hours. You can also freeze it overnight. (Because of the alcohol content, it will not freeze to a solid state.)

3. Use a fork to break up the semi-frozen mixture and put it in the blender. Blend on high speed until it has a smooth and creamy consistency. Serve immediately, garnished with a strawberry if desired. Leftover frosé can be frozen for up to a week and blended again before serving.

*Note: You can use your choice of wine and berries. Secco brand wine is a good low-carb choice.*

NET CARBS 1.1g

| calories | fat | protein | carbs | fiber |
|---|---|---|---|---|
| 79 | 0.2g | 0.4g | 4.6g | 3.5g |

# Sangria

yield: six 8-ounce servings • prep time: 15 minutes, plus 4 hours to chill

1 (750-ml) bottle dry red wine

¼ cup granular sweetener

½ cup blueberries

½ cup sliced strawberries

1 lemon, sliced, plus more for garnish

1 lime, sliced, plus more for garnish

2 teaspoons pure orange extract

½ cup vodka

1 (12-ounce) can orange sparkling water

Ice, for serving

1. Pour the wine into a 2-quart pitcher. Add the sweetener, berries, lemon slices, lime slices, and orange extract. Use a muddler or the back of a wooden spoon to muddle the ingredients until the sweetener is dissolved. Stir in the vodka. For the best flavor, cover and refrigerate for at least 4 hours.

2. Stir in the sparkling water just before serving. Serve over ice, garnished with more lemon and lime slices. Leftover sangria can be stored, covered, in the refrigerator for up to 3 days.

NET CARBS 6.5g

| calories | fat | protein | carbs | fiber |
|---|---|---|---|---|
| 119 | 0.2g | 0.5g | 7.7g | 1.2g |

# Blackberry Mojito

yield: one 8-ounce serving • prep time: 10 minutes

3 fresh mint leaves, plus more for garnish

2 tablespoons freshly squeezed lime juice

8 blackberries, plus more for garnish

1 teaspoon granular sweetener

¼ cup white rum

Ice, for serving

6 ounces club soda

1 lime wedge, for garnish

1. Place the mint, lime juice, blackberries, and sweetener in a 12-ounce glass. Use a muddler or the back of a wooden spoon to muddle the mint and blackberries until the sweetener is dissolved.

2. Stir in the rum and fill the glass with ice. Pour in the club soda and gently stir. Garnish with blackberries, mint, and a lime wedge.

*Note: You can simply leave out the alcohol for a great-tasting mocktail.*

NET CARBS 2.7g

| calories | fat | protein | carbs | fiber |
|----------|-----|---------|-------|-------|
| 155 | 0.3g | 0.8g | 6.7g | 4g |

# Frozen Strawberry Margaritas

yield: four 12-ounce servings • prep time: 15 minutes

**Kosher-size salt**

**½ cup freshly squeezed lime juice**

**½ cup silver tequila**

**2 teaspoons pure orange extract**

**2 tablespoons confectioners' sweetener**

**½ cup sliced strawberries**

**4 cups ice, plus more if needed**

For Garnish:

**4 lime wedges**

**4 strawberries**

1. Pour a thin layer of kosher-size salt onto a small plate. Moisten the rims of four 12-ounce glasses with some of the lime juice, then dip each one into the salt. Set the rimmed glasses aside.

2. Place the remaining lime juice, tequila, orange extract, sweetener, strawberries, and ice in a blender. Blend on high speed until smooth. Add more ice if needed to thicken. Serve immediately in the rimmed glasses, each garnished with a lime wedge and a strawberry.

NET CARBS 3.9g

| calories | fat | protein | carbs | fiber |
|---|---|---|---|---|
| 85 | 0.2g | 0.3g | 4.5g | 0.6g |

*Chapter 8*

## Seasonings, Dressings & Other Basics

# Blackening Seasoning

yield: ½ cup (1 tablespoon per serving) · prep time: 5 minutes

**2 tablespoons smoked paprika**

**1 tablespoon brown sugar substitute**

**1 tablespoon salt**

**1 tablespoon ground black pepper**

**2 teaspoons cayenne pepper**

**1 teaspoon garlic powder**

**1 teaspoon onion powder**

**1 teaspoon dried basil**

**1 teaspoon ground dried oregano**

**½ teaspoon dried thyme leaves**

In a small bowl, stir all of the ingredients together until well combined. Store in a jar with a lid. Shake before use.

*Note: This seasoning is a key ingredient in my Blackened Salmon recipe (page 180). It's also delicious on a variety of other meats and seafood, from shrimp to chicken to pork chops and steaks.*

NET CARBS 1.4g

| calories | fat | protein | carbs | fiber |
|----------|-----|---------|-------|-------|
| 12 | 0.3g | 0.5g | 2.5g | 1.2g |

# Ranch Seasoning

yield: about 1 cup (1 tablespoon per serving) · prep time: 5 minutes

**5 tablespoons dried parsley leaves**

**3 tablespoons dried dill weed**

**2 tablespoons dried chives**

**2 tablespoons garlic powder**

**1 tablespoon dried minced onions**

**1 tablespoon onion powder**

**2 teaspoons salt**

**2 teaspoons ground black pepper**

In a small bowl, stir all of the ingredients together until well combined. Store in a jar with a lid. Shake before use.

*Note: Ranch seasoning is easier to make than you might think, and it's so much better than store-bought. In this book, I use it to give the Buffalo Shrimp & Ranch Cauli-Rice recipe (page 162) its signature flavor and, of course, to make Ranch Dressing (page 268). You'll find other uses for it in my previous cookbook, Southern Keto.*

NET CARBS 1.2g

| calories | fat | protein | carbs | fiber |
|---|---|---|---|---|
| 8 | 0.1g | 0.4g | 1.7g | 0.4g |

# Ranch Dressing

yield: about 2 cups (¼ cup per serving) · prep time: 5 minutes

1 cup sour cream

½ cup mayonnaise

¼ cup heavy cream, plus more if needed

1 teaspoon freshly squeezed lemon juice

2 tablespoons Ranch Seasoning (page 267)

In a small bowl, stir the ingredients together until completely blended. If the dressing is too thick, thin it with more cream, adding 1 teaspoon at a time. Store in an airtight container in the refrigerator for up to a week.

*Note: If you own my previous book, you will recognize this recipe. Ranch dressing is so fundamental that it deserves to be repeated here; this book would not be complete without it! Two of my favorite recipes in this book to pair with ranch dressing are the Dill Pickle Poppers (page 76) and the Crispy Buffalo Shrimp (page 94).*

NET CARBS 3.5g

| calories | fat | protein | carbs | fiber |
|----------|------|---------|-------|-------|
| 334 | 35.3g | 2g | 3.8g | 0.2g |

# Poppy Seed Dressing

yield: ⅔ cup (¼ cup per serving) · prep time: 5 minutes

⅓ cup extra-virgin olive oil

¼ cup granular sweetener

2 tablespoons apple cider vinegar

2 teaspoons poppy seeds

1 teaspoon ground mustard

¼ teaspoon freshly ground black pepper

⅛ teaspoon salt

In a small bowl, whisk together all of the ingredients. Store in a jar with a lid in the refrigerator for up to a week. Shake before using. If the dressing becomes too thick, thin it with water, adding 1 teaspoon at a time, until the consistency is to your liking.

*Note: This is the classic choice for a Strawberry Spinach Salad (page 108). But there's no need to limit yourself to spinach; this dressing is delicious served over a variety of greens, such as arugula, iceberg lettuce, leaf lettuce, and romaine lettuce.*

NET CARBS 0.5g

| calories | fat | protein | carbs | fiber |
|----------|-----|---------|-------|-------|
| 256 | 28.1g | 0.6g | 1.1g | 0.5g |

# Berry Vinaigrette

yield: 1½ cups (¼ cup per serving) · prep time: 10 minutes

**8 ounces fresh berries of choice**

**3 tablespoons extra-virgin olive oil**

**2 tablespoons red wine vinegar**

**1 tablespoon granular sweetener**

**¼ teaspoon salt**

Place all of the ingredients in a blender or food processor and blend until smooth. Store in a jar with a lid in the refrigerator for up to a week. Shake before using. If the dressing gets too thick after refrigerating, thin it with a few drops of water.

*Note: I was inspired to create this recipe when craving summer salads. It's a great dressing for mixed greens, and a great choice for a side salad meant to accompany anything smoky or spicy, like barbecue or Blackened Salmon (page 180).*

NET CARBS 2.4g

| calories | fat | protein | carbs | fiber |
|----------|-----|---------|-------|-------|
| 79 | 7g | 0.4g | 4g | 1.6g |

# Roasted Tomato Marinara

yield: 1½ cups (¼ cup per serving) • prep time: 10 minutes • cook time: 35 minutes

**2 pints cherry tomatoes**

**½ onion, sliced**

**3 cloves garlic, sliced**

**2 tablespoons extra-virgin olive oil**

**1 teaspoon chopped fresh basil leaves**

**½ teaspoon ground dried oregano**

**½ teaspoon ground black pepper**

**¼ teaspoon salt**

1. Preheat the oven to 425°F. Line a sheet pan with parchment paper.

2. Put the tomatoes, onion, and garlic in the prepared pan. Drizzle with the oil, then sprinkle the basil, oregano, pepper, and salt evenly over the top. Gently toss to coat the tomatoes in the oil and seasonings.

3. Roast the tomatoes for 25 to 35 minutes, until soft and fragrant. Allow to cool completely.

4. Transfer the roasted tomatoes, onion, and garlic to a blender. Pulse and blend until the sauce is smooth. It will be thick; you can add 1 tablespoon of oil and 1 tablespoon of water at a time to thin it to your desired consistency. Add more salt to taste, if desired. Store in an airtight container in the refrigerator for up to 5 days.

*Note: This sauce is delicious served over spaghetti squash or zucchini noodles. Whenever a recipe in this book calls for marinara sauce, you can use this homemade version instead of store-bought. It will make those dishes extra tasty.*

NET CARBS 4.8g

| calories | fat | protein | carbs | fiber |
|----------|-----|---------|-------|-------|
| 80 | 5.2g | 4.4g | 7.5g | 2.9g |

# Teriyaki Sauce

yield: ½ cup (2 tablespoons per serving) • prep time: 5 minutes • cook time: 15 minutes

½ cup coconut aminos or gluten-free soy sauce

¼ cup water

¼ cup brown sugar substitute

2 tablespoons sugar-free maple syrup

½ teaspoon ginger powder

¼ teaspoon garlic powder

5 drops liquid stevia

¼ teaspoon xanthan gum

½ teaspoon pure orange extract

1. Put the aminos, water, brown sugar substitute, maple syrup, ginger powder, garlic powder, and stevia in a small saucepan. Bring to a simmer over medium heat, whisking occasionally, then, while whisking, sprinkle the mixture with the xanthan gum. Once the xanthan gum is incorporated, reduce the heat to low. Allow the sauce to simmer, stirring occasionally, until it starts to thicken, about 10 minutes.

2. Remove the pan from the heat and stir in the orange extract. The sauce will continue to thicken as it cools. Allow to completely cool before using. Store in an airtight container in the refrigerator for up to a week.

*Note: This sauce makes a great marinade for beef, chicken, or pork and is delicious with vegetables such as broccoli and green beans. It can be used in any recipe that calls for teriyaki sauce. In this book, it is used in the Teriyaki Pork Chops (page 182).*

NET CARBS 2.3g

| calories | fat | protein | carbs | fiber |
|----------|------|---------|-------|-------|
| 27 | 0.4g | 0g | 2.4g | 0.2g |

# Buffalo Sauce

yield: about 1½ cups (¼ cup per serving) · prep time: 5 minutes · cook time: 5 minutes

**½ cup (1 stick) salted butter**

**1 cup hot sauce, room temperature (see Note)**

**Ground black pepper**

Melt the butter in a small saucepan over medium-low heat. Stir in the hot sauce. Stir continuously until the butter and hot sauce are completely combined. Season with pepper to taste. Remove from the heat and allow to cool for 10 minutes before serving. Store in an airtight container in the refrigerator for up to 2 weeks. Stir before using.

*Note: When making this recipe, it's important to use room-temperature hot sauce so that the ingredients blend well. A medium-hot hot sauce, such as Frank's RedHot, is ideal. Whenever a recipe in this book calls for Buffalo sauce, you can use this homemade version instead of store-bought.*

NET CARBS 0g

| calories | fat | protein | carbs | fiber |
|----------|-----|---------|-------|-------|
| 136 | 15.4g | 0.2g | 0g | 0g |

# Sugar-Free Raspberry Jam

yield: ½ cup (2 tablespoons per serving) · prep time: 5 minutes · cook time: 20 minutes

**1 cup raspberries**

**¼ cup granulated sweetener**

**1 teaspoon freshly squeezed lemon juice**

1. In a medium-size saucepan over medium heat, bring the raspberries and sweetener to a boil. Mash the berries as they cook.

2. Stir in the lemon juice and reduce the heat to medium-low. Allow the jam to simmer, stirring frequently, until thickened, about 15 minutes.

3. Remove the pan from the heat and allow the jam to cool. It will thicken further as it cools. Store in a glass jar with a lid in the refrigerator for up to 2 weeks.

*Note: Use this jam for Baked Raspberry Walnut Brie (page 90). It's also great as a topping for yogurt, low-carb biscuits, or toast.*

NET CARBS 3g

| calories | fat | protein | carbs | fiber |
|----------|------|---------|-------|-------|
| 21 | 0.2g | 0.4g | 5g | 2g |

# Sweetened Condensed Milk

yield: 1½ cups (¼ cup per serving) · prep time: 5 minutes · cook time: 35 minutes

2 cups heavy cream

3 tablespoons salted butter

½ cup confectioners' sweetener

1 teaspoon pure vanilla extract

In a medium-size saucepan over medium-low heat, whisk together the cream, butter, and sweetener. Bring the mixture to a low boil, stirring every minute to keep it from boiling over; keep an eye on it! Lower the heat and allow to simmer for 30 minutes, until the mixture has thickened and reduced by about one-third. Stir in the vanilla. Remove the pan from the heat and allow to cool completely before using; the milk will continue to thicken as it cools. Store in a glass jar with a lid in the refrigerator for up to a week.

*Note: Sweetened condensed milk is a key ingredient in my Magic Layer Bars (page 244), but don't feel restricted to that recipe. This keto version can be used in any recipe that calls for sweetened condensed milk. You can use it in cakes, pies, fudge, and anything else you've missed because you didn't have a low-carb option for sweetened condensed milk.*

NET CARBS 0.7g

| calories | fat | protein | carbs | fiber |
|----------|-----|---------|-------|-------|
| 321 | 32.4g | 2.7g | 0.7g | 0g |

# Graham Cracker Crust

yield: one 9-inch crust (8 servings) · prep time: 10 minutes
cook time: 15 minutes

**1½ cups finely ground blanched almond flour**

**2 tablespoons brown sugar substitute**

**2 teaspoons ground cinnamon**

**⅛ teaspoon salt**

**¼ cup (½ stick) cold salted butter, sliced**

**1 teaspoon sugar-free maple syrup**

**1 teaspoon pure vanilla extract**

1. Preheat the oven to 325°F. Grease a 9-inch pie plate with oil or butter.

2. In a medium-size mixing bowl, whisk together the almond flour, brown sugar substitute, cinnamon, and salt. Add the butter, maple syrup, and vanilla and use a pastry blender or fork to break up the butter until the mixture resembles coarse crumbs.

3. Using your hands, press the dough evenly across the bottom and up the sides of the prepared pie plate. Use a fork to lightly prick the bottom of the crust several times.

4. Bake for 12 to 15 minutes, until light golden brown. Let cool before filling.

*Note: This crust is for refrigerator pies. If you'd like to use it for a baked pie, I suggest baking the crust for a few minutes less so it doesn't become too brown.*

| calories | fat | protein | carbs | fiber |
|---|---|---|---|---|
| 165 | 15.6g | 4.1g | 4.1g | 2.2g |

NET CARBS 1.9g

# ❈ Gratitude ❈

Thank you to all of the people in my life who made this book possible. I'm blessed with the best support system of family and friends.

Thank you to the amazing team at Victory Belt for believing in me, taking a chance on me the first time, and encouraging me to write another book! I appreciate you so much.

Thank you to my husband and children for always supporting my dreams and being my rock. I'm so thankful I get to do life with you, and I love you with all of my heart.

Thanks to my mom and dad for always believing in me and loving me unconditionally. You gave me the best foundation, and for that I'm thankful. We are so glad you live close to us now!

# ❊ Testimonials ❊

I have struggled with obesity my entire life. I've tried every fad diet in the books and even took diet pills, only seeing short-term success. It was always the same old story: gain the weight back plus some once I stopped taking the pills. My motivation or "why" was that my husband and I were having trouble getting pregnant. When my gynecologist looked me in the face and gave me the harsh reality that my weight was holding me back, I knew right then and there that I wasn't going to keep letting my addiction of unhealthy foods/habits hold me back from living my life!

I did the typical cliche thing and joined a gym on January 1, 2009, cleaned out our pantry/fridge, and replaced everything with healthy/low-carb options. Through eating low-carb/whole foods and exercising 7 days a week for 6 months, I lost 85 pounds. I was able to maintain that weight loss over the years, even while having two children in the process.

However, in 2018 I began to get a little comfortable/going back to old unhealthy habits of eating. This slowly resulted in the weight coming back on. It was the influence of a friend doing keto that sparked my interest in the lifestyle. Keto was more strict, but looked very familiar to what I had done to lose the initial weight. In January 2019 (again cliche, I know!), I decided to take a chance and get my life back on a healthy track.

I will admit, starting keto was overwhelming—so many different types of keto, ingredients, recipes, and opinions! The first month I did a ton of research for recipes that were close to what I was used to eating here in southern Louisiana. I just thought, "There has to be some Southern copycat recipes for keto!" This is one time Google didn't steer me wrong! I found Natasha's *Southern Keto* cookbook. I couldn't believe how the recipes I loved could still be keto! From Natasha's blueberry muffins to her drop biscuits and gravy, I fell in love with the keto lifestyle! Natasha and a few other keto cooks inspired me to play around with recipes and create a cookbook of my own.

With the help of Natasha's recipes, I have lost 25 pounds living a ketogenic lifestyle. I never feel deprived or that this is a diet! I'm currently in maintenance mode/building muscle at this point in my journey; however, I am inspired by Natasha and her creativity in the kitchen. She makes every recipe easy and keeps the ingredients simple, which I appreciate. I'm so excited to add more delicious recipes to my keto lifestyle arsenal! Thank you, Natasha, you're the absolute best!!

Nicole Burgess
@npburgess184 on Instagram

The keto diet changed my life. It changed how I felt about myself and for five-plus years has given me a true freedom around food that I cannot explain other than it gave me parameters that I can sustain long term.

I have struggled with my weight for my entire life. I have tried every diet from the popcorn diet to Jenny Craig to the cabbage soup diet. I would lose weight, but as soon as I finished the "diet," the weight would begin to come back on because I had no education around what I was doing. I didn't realize I needed to change my life and relationship with food until I found keto.

After finishing up what seemed to be my hundredth attempt to lose weight and try to control my PCOS symptoms and have a baby without success, I searched "diets for infertility and PCOS," and keto popped up. I had never heard of keto, but after doing one page of "research," I decided eating meat and cheese was for sure something I could do! I didn't tell anyone and just started doing that: eating meat and cheese. After a month, I had lost 10 pounds *but* I felt amazing.

After more research and after sticking to a "diet" with success for the first time in my life, but not feeling the weight of a diet, just feeling like I was eating, I knew this was what I needed to do long term. Of course, I broadened my food groups to include vegetables, berries, and some good-for-you foods and fell in love with this easy, sustainable way of eating.

I had been taking 1500 mg of metformin (three huge horse pills!) to control my PCOS, and after six months of eating the keto diet, my doctor called to tell me that all my levels were within the normal range and I would stop all medication. The medicine made my stomach hurt all the time, and I cannot tell you what a relief it was to be able to control PCOS with food.

What started as another diet to lose weight led me to so many more good things. I have been eating the ketogenic diet for almost six years. I lost 70 pounds and kept it off, had a little girl, and still am eating my way through the meat aisle at the grocery store, content with the food freedom I found with keto.

It is doable if you make it easy. It is sustainable if you make it easy. Tools like *Southern Keto* make everyday keto a treat instead of a chore. One of my favorite things is to find a meal I love that is heavy with carbohydrates and make it low-carb and then look at my husband over dinner with a mouthful of great-for-my-body fuel and say, "You know, this is really good!"

If you think keto is too hard for you or is something you can't do, trust me when I tell you that you can do this. Take a simple approach; don't over-research it. Don't make it 100 steps to a beautiful meal. Follow the beautiful pages of this book. Natasha is so wise, and her recipes are some of my go-tos (and I even have a cookbook!) because they are delicious and you don't even realize you are eating keto because it is just good food. Southern gals now how to cook, let me tell you! And lastly remember, this actually IS something you can do to change your life. Stay consistent, don't stress about weight loss, and focus on how good you feel. Keto truly changed my life. I can look back over the last six years and some of the biggest blessings in my life are because I started on a Keto journey and my hope is that you can feel that as well.

Jessica Dukes
@jessicadukesdaily on Instagram

I have been overweight most of my adult life, and every year, my weight just kept going higher and higher. I had heard so many great weight loss stories from people doing keto, so I thought I would try it out. Losing weight was my only goal at that point, but then I started noticing other things happening as well. I could tell a *huge* difference in my energy level. I used to have to take one- to two-hour naps *daily* just to function. I no longer need to do this. I have energy to stay awake the entire day. I would also get out of breath just walking up stairs, but now I can go up them several times in a row and not be winded! This way of eating has definitely helped reduce inflammation in my body. I used to be sore for days after walking around the block, but now I can walk for miles and not be in pain.

So far, I have lost over 80 pounds by living a ketogenic lifestyle, but I have reached so many other non-scale victories. I was shocked when I realized I could cross my legs easily and could bend over and tie my shoes without turning my foot sideways. It sounds kind of silly, but I could not do so many "daily routine" activities because of my weight. I have so much more stamina now, and I can do so many things that I used to have to put off until I felt better (which was usually never). After over 20 years of not wearing shorts in the summertime in Texas, I have worn them almost every day since the summer of 2019.

Before keto, I was borderline diabetic. I hated going to see my doctor because he would preach to me about needing to lose weight, and he prescribed so many medications and would tell me I needed to exercise. I no longer dread going to see him because, through keto, my A1c has lowered to 5.1 and my triglycerides have dropped over 100 points! I am no longer on any prescription medications.

Along my keto journey, I bought cookbooks. One of them was *Southern Keto.* This book made it so much easier to cook food that my whole family can enjoy. I can make biscuits, casseroles, soups, holiday meals, appetizers, and desserts using this book, and I almost always have all the ingredients on hand. Cooking from scratch made an even bigger difference in my quest for health. Another non-scale victory is the money and time I have saved by not going out to eat as often as I used to do. I enjoy cooking the food myself and knowing all the ingredients that go into it. I have learned how to cook so many new things but also how to revamp family favorites. Thank you to Natasha and all the other recipe creators out there, because you help make our lives (and meals) better!

Polica McCauley
@keto_polica on Instagram


Before I found the keto diet, I was sad, angry, and lost. I didn't know how much my diet and my life revolving around food was holding me back. I found keto and gave it a shot. This was before it was the cool new thing, and honestly, no one knew if it even worked! Here I am, five years and 70 pounds less, and I know that without my keto lifestyle, I wouldn't be where I am today! Keto is a great weight loss tool, and I wouldn't be the person I am today without my keto knowledge and daily work to be a happier, healthier human.

Samantha Marpé
@keto.sam.iam on Instagram

# ☀ Measurement & Cooking ☀ Conversion Tables

### LIQUIDS

| | |
|---|---|
| ¼ teaspoon | 1.25 ml |
| ½ teaspoon | 2.5 ml |
| 1 teaspoon | 5 ml |
| 1 tablespoon | 15 ml |
| ¼ cup | 60 ml |
| ⅓ cup | 80 ml |
| ½ cup | 125 ml |
| 1 cup | 250 ml |

### DRY INGREDIENTS

| | |
|---|---|
| 1 oz | 28 g |
| 2 oz | 55 g |
| 3 oz | 85 g |
| 4 oz | 115 g |
| 8 oz | 225 g |
| 12 oz | 340 g |
| 16 oz / 1 pound | 455 g |
| 32 oz | 907 g |

### TEMPERATURE

| | |
|---|---|
| 275°F | 140°C |
| 300°F | 150°C |
| 325°F | 170°C |
| 350°F | 180°C |
| 375°F | 190°C |
| 400°F | 200°C |
| 425°F | 220°C |
| 450°F | 230°C |

# ❊ Resources ❊

## Favorite Products

These are just a few of the great keto products that I enjoy. The keto market has exploded in the last couple of years, and there's no way to include them all. It's also good to keep in mind that the popularity of keto has brought about a lot of new products, and they aren't all equal in ingredients and quality. Do your own research, and always read labels.

### ChocZero

choczero.com
Delicious keto-friendly chocolate syrups and more. They offer a variety of chocolate chip flavors, chocolate bars, and many flavors of syrups.

### Defy Foods

defyfoods.com
After losing a combined 150 pounds with keto, best friends Suzanne and Jessica launched Defy Foods, a low-carb and keto food company. Their first product is a deliciously crunchy gluten-free cracker with only 2 grams of net carbs per serving.

### Good Dee's

gooddees.com
A delicious variety of low-carb and gluten-free baking mixes for cookies, cakes, and more. Also available on Amazon.com.

### Heka

hekagoodfoods.com
Ketogenic-certified bars and cookies that are made with clean ingredients and come in a variety of flavors, many containing only 1 gram of net carbs per serving.

### Hilo

hilolife.com
Keto-friendly bold crunchy cheese and nut snack mixes. Also available on Amazon.com.

### Kawaii Treats and Eats

kawaiitreatsandeats.com
Great-tasting gluten-free, sugar-free, and keto-friendly baking mixes with ingredients you can feel good about.

### KetoKrate

ketokrate.com
A monthly keto snack subscription box. A fun way to sample new keto products without committing to large quantities.

## Lakanto

**lakanto.com**
A variety of monkfruit-sweetened products. Lakanto uses a blend of monkfruit and erythritol. They also make a brown sugar substitute. These products can sometimes be found at Costco.

## LUV Ice Cream

**luvicecream.net**
If you find yourself in Saint Paul, Minnesota, visit this charming keto-friendly ice cream shop! They have wonderful keto ice cream and homemade baked goods. They even make their own chocolate in house! A variety of products can be purchased on the LUV website; find their chocolate chips on Amazon.com.

## Nush

**nushfoods.com**
Keto-friendly snack cakes and cookies made with clean ingredients.

## Ratio

**ratiofood.com**
Crunchy protein bars and creamy keto-friendly dairy snacks. Can be found in some grocery stores.

## Secco Wine

**seccowineclub.com**
Keto- and Paleo-friendly low-carb wines, most with less than 1 gram of carbs per glass. The world's first wine with a nutrition label. You don't need a subscription to purchase it.

## Southern Recipe Small Batch

**southernrecipesmallbatch.com**
Gluten-free pork rind snacks that come in a wide variety of unique flavors. World Market and some grocery stores carry these.

# Books

*The Art and Science of Low Carbohydrate Living* by Jeff S. Volek, PhD, RD, and Stephen D. Phinney, MD, PhD

*End Your Carb Confusion* by Eric C. Westman, MD, and Amy Berger, CNS

*Keto Clarity* by Jimmy Moore and Eric C. Westman, MD

# Recipe Quick Reference

| RECIPE | PAGE | 🌰 | ⊘ | 🥛 | ⏱30 |
|---|---|---|---|---|---|
| Maple Brown Sugar N'oatmeal | 46 | | ✓ | ✓ | ✓ |
| Breakfast Pizza Casserole | 48 | ✓ | | | |
| Cinnamon Pull-Apart Bread | 50 | | | | |
| Breakfast Sandwich "Buns" | 52 | ✓ | | | ✓ |
| Blueberry Lemon Coffee Cake | 54 | | | | |
| Grain-Free Granola Bars | 56 | | | ✓ | ✓ |
| Strawberry Breakfast Cake | 58 | | | | |
| Low-Carb Banana Bread | 60 | | | | |
| Jalapeño Cheddar Scones | 62 | | | | |
| Bacon Pimento Cheese Muffins | 64 | | | | ✓ |
| Caramelized Onion & Bacon Frittata | 66 | ✓ | | | |
| "Apple" Pie Muffins | 68 | | | | |
| Savory Skillet Zucchini Bread | 70 | | | | |
| Jalapeño Popper Dip | 74 | ✓ | ✓ | | |
| Dill Pickle Poppers | 76 | ✓ | ✓ | | ✓ |
| Spicy Sweet Almonds | 78 | | | ✓ | ✓ |
| Shrimp Spread with Parmesan Crisps | 80 | ✓ | | | |
| Pizza Dip | 82 | ✓ | ✓ | | ✓ |
| Deviled Ham | 84 | ✓ | | | |
| Low-Carb Onion Rings | 86 | ✓ | | | ✓ |
| Stuffed Banana Peppers | 88 | ✓ | ✓ | | |
| Baked Raspberry Walnut Brie | 90 | | ✓ | | ✓ |
| Everything Crackers | 92 | | | | ✓ |
| Crispy Buffalo Shrimp | 94 | ✓ | | | |
| Pecan-Encrusted Tuna Ball | 96 | | ✓ | | |
| Spicy Ranch Dip | 98 | ✓ | | | |
| Roasted Red Pepper Hummus | 100 | | ✓ | ✓ | |
| Sweet & Salty Snack Mix | 102 | | ✓ | | ✓ |
| Maple Dijon Broccoli Slaw | 106 | | ✓ | ✓ | |
| Strawberry Spinach Salad | 108 | | ✓ | ✓ | ✓ |
| Asian Coleslaw | 110 | | ✓ | ✓ | |
| Layered Summer Salad | 112 | ✓ | | | |
| Antipasto Salad with Creamy Italian Dressing | 114 | ✓ | | | ✓ |
| Zuppa Toscana | 116 | ✓ | ✓ | | |
| Unstuffed Pepper Soup | 118 | ✓ | ✓ | ○ | |

| RECIPE | PAGE | 🥜 | ⊘ | 🥛 | 30 |
|---|---|---|---|---|---|
| French Onion Soup | 120 | | ✓ | | |
| Green Chile Chicken Soup | 122 | ✓ | ✓ | | |
| Easy Buffalo Chicken Soup | 124 | ✓ | ✓ | | |
| Sheet Pan Zucchini Pizza Bake | 128 | ✓ | ✓ | | |
| Salisbury Steak | 130 | ✓ | | | |
| Sheet Pan Smoked Sausage & Cabbage | 132 | ✓ | ✓ | ✓ | |
| Country Fried Steak & Gravy | 134 | ✓ | | | ✓ |
| Garlic Parmesan Shrimp | 136 | ✓ | ✓ | | ✓ |
| Zucchini Parmesan | 138 | ✓ | | | |
| Meatball Marinara | 140 | ✓ | | | |
| Shepherd's Pie | 142 | ✓ | ✓ | | |
| Ground Beef Teriyaki Bowl | 144 | ✓ | ✓ | ✓ | ✓ |
| Shrimp Alfredo Spaghetti Squash | 146 | ✓ | ✓ | | |
| Lump Crab Cakes with Chipotle Mayo | 148 | ✓ | | | |
| Bacon Cheeseburger Cauli-Rice Skillet | 150 | ✓ | | | |
| Pork Fried Rice | 152 | ✓ | | ✓ | ✓ |
| Brown Sugar–Glazed Meatloaf | 154 | ✓ | | ✓ | |
| Sheet Pan Smoked Sausage & Peppers | 156 | ✓ | ✓ | ✓ | |
| Corn Dog Casserole | 158 | | | | |
| Roast Beef & Caramelized Onion Pizza | 160 | | | | |
| Buffalo Shrimp & Ranch Cauli-Rice | 162 | ✓ | | | |
| Cheesy Green Chile Pork Chops | 164 | ✓ | ✓ | | |
| Lasagna-Stuffed Spaghetti Squash | 166 | ✓ | ✓ | | |
| Chicken & Dumpling Casserole | 168 | | | | |
| Nashville Hot Chicken Tenders | 170 | ✓ | | | |
| Meatza | 172 | ✓ | | | |
| Slow Cooker Chicken Tacos | 174 | ✓ | ✓ | | |
| Fiesta Casserole | 176 | ✓ | ✓ | | |
| Shrimp & Andouille Sausage Jambalaya | 178 | ✓ | ✓ | | |
| Blackened Salmon | 180 | ✓ | ✓ | | ✓ |
| Teriyaki Pork Chops | 182 | ✓ | ✓ | ✓ | |
| Reuben Wraps | 184 | ✓ | | | ✓ |
| Slow Cooker Cheesesteak Pot Roast | 186 | ✓ | ✓ | | |
| Crispy Fried Brussels Sprouts | 190 | ✓ | ✓ | ✓ | ✓ |
| Smashed Radishes | 192 | ✓ | ✓ | | |
| Roasted Cheesy Cauli-Mac | 194 | ✓ | ✓ | | |
| Mushroom Cauli-Risotto | 196 | ✓ | ✓ | | |
| Prosciutto Provolone Asparagus | 198 | ✓ | ✓ | | ✓ |
| Asiago Roasted Green Beans | 200 | ✓ | ✓ | | |
| Cilantro Lime Cauli-Rice | 202 | ✓ | ✓ | | ✓ |

| RECIPE | PAGE | 🌰 | ⊘ | 🍶 | ⏱30 |
|---|---|---|---|---|---|
| Spaghetti Squash Fritters | 204 | ✓ | | | |
| Southern Summer Squash Casserole | 206 | ✓ | | | |
| Sheet Pan Parmesan Yellow Squash & Zucchini | 208 | ✓ | ✓ | | ✓ |
| Roasted Garlic Chive Cauli-Mash | 210 | ✓ | ✓ | | |
| Zucchini Carrot Cake | 214 | | | | |
| Salted Dark Chocolate Almond Bark | 216 | | ✓ | | |
| Lemon Cheesecake Mousse | 218 | ✓ | ✓ | | |
| Loaded N'oatmeal Cookies | 220 | | | | |
| Edible Cookie Dough | 222 | | ✓ | | |
| No-Bake Strawberry Cream Pie | 224 | | ✓ | | |
| German Chocolate Cake | 226 | | | | |
| Muddy Buddies | 228 | | ✓ | | ✓ |
| Peanut Butter Pie with Chocolate Crust | 230 | | ✓ | | |
| Skillet Blondie for Two | 232 | | | ○ | ✓ |
| Peanut Butter Cup Bars | 234 | | ✓ | | |
| Lisa's Peanut Butter Cheesecake Brownies | 236 | | | | |
| Toasted Coconut Bars | 238 | ✓ | ✓ | | |
| Chocolate Cookie Crumbs | 240 | | ✓ | | ✓ |
| Dirt Cake | 242 | | ✓ | | |
| Magic Layer Bars | 244 | | ✓ | | |
| Banana Cream Pie | 246 | | ✓ | | |
| Toasted Coconut Custard | 248 | ✓ | | | |
| Red Velvet Cake | 250 | | | | |
| Forgotten Cookies | 252 | | | ✓ | |
| Strawberry-Infused Lemonade | 254 | ✓ | ✓ | ✓ | |
| Frosé | 256 | ✓ | ✓ | ✓ | |
| Sangria | 258 | ✓ | ✓ | ✓ | |
| Blackberry Mojito | 260 | ✓ | ✓ | ✓ | ✓ |
| Frozen Strawberry Margaritas | 262 | ✓ | ✓ | ✓ | ✓ |
| Blackening Seasoning | 266 | ✓ | ✓ | ✓ | ✓ |
| Ranch Seasoning | 267 | ✓ | ✓ | ✓ | ✓ |
| Ranch Dressing | 268 | ✓ | | | ✓ |
| Poppy Seed Dressing | 269 | ✓ | ✓ | ✓ | ✓ |
| Berry Vinaigrette | 270 | ✓ | ✓ | ✓ | ✓ |
| Roasted Tomato Marinara | 271 | ✓ | ✓ | ✓ | |
| Teriyaki Sauce | 272 | ✓ | ✓ | ✓ | ✓ |
| Buffalo Sauce | 273 | ✓ | ✓ | | ✓ |
| Sugar-Free Raspberry Jam | 274 | ✓ | ✓ | ✓ | ✓ |
| Sweetened Condensed Milk | 275 | ✓ | ✓ | | |
| Graham Cracker Crust | 276 | | ✓ | | ✓ |

# ❊ Recipe Index ❊

## Breakfast & Breads

46

**Maple Brown Sugar N'oatmeal**

48

**Breakfast Pizza Casserole**

50

**Cinnamon Pull-Apart Bread**

52

**Breakfast Sandwich "Buns"**

54

**Blueberry Lemon Coffee Cake**

56

**Grain-Free Granola Bars**

58

**Strawberry Breakfast Cake**

60

**Low-Carb Banana Bread**

62

**Jalapeño Cheddar Scones**

64

**Bacon Pimento Cheese Muffins**

66

**Caramelized Onion & Bacon Frittata**

68

**"Apple" Pie Muffins**

70

**Savory Skillet Zucchini Bread**

# Appetizers & Snacks

| | | |
|---|---|---|
| **74** Jalapeño Popper Dip | **76** Dill Pickle Poppers | **78** Spicy Sweet Almonds |
| **80** Shrimp Spread with Parmesan Crisps | **82** Pizza Dip | |

Jalapeño Popper Dip

Dill Pickle Poppers

Spicy Sweet Almonds

Shrimp Spread with Parmesan Crisps

Pizza Dip

Deviled Ham

Low-Carb Onion Rings

Stuffed Banana Peppers

Baked Raspberry Walnut Brie

Everything Crackers

Crispy Buffalo Shrimp

Pecan-Encrusted Tuna Ball

Spicy Ranch Dip

Roasted Red Pepper Hummus

Sweet & Salty Snack Mix

# Soups & Salads

**106** Maple Dijon Broccoli Slaw

**108** Strawberry Spinach Salad

**110** Asian Coleslaw

**112** Layered Summer Salad

**114** Antipasto Salad with Creamy Italian Dressing

**116** Zuppa Toscana

**118** Unstuffed Pepper Soup

**120** French Onion Soup

**122** Green Chile Chicken Soup

**124** Easy Buffalo Chicken Soup

# Main Dishes

*128*

Sheet Pan
Zucchini
Pizza Bake

*130*

Salisbury Steak

*132*

Sheet Pan Smoked
Sausage & Cabbage

*134*

Country Fried
Steak & Gravy

*136*

Garlic Parmesan
Shrimp

*138*

Zucchini
Parmesan

*140*

Meatball Marinara

*142*

Shepherd's Pie

*144*

Ground Beef
Teriyaki Bowl

*146*

Shrimp Alfredo
Spaghetti Squash

*148*

Lump Crab Cakes
with Chipotle
Mayo

*150*

Bacon
Cheeseburger
Cauli-Rice Skillet

*152*

Pork Fried Rice

*154*

Brown Sugar-
Glazed Meatloaf

*156*

Sheet Pan Smoked
Sausage & Peppers

*158*

Corn Dog
Casserole

*160*

Roast Beef &
Caramelized
Onion Pizza

*162*

Buffalo Shrimp &
Ranch Cauli-Rice

*164*

Cheesy Green
Chile Pork Chops

*166*

Lasagna-Stuffed
Spaghetti Squash

*168*

Chicken &
Dumpling
Casserole

*170*

Nashville Hot
Chicken Tenders

*172*

Meatza

*174*

Slow Cooker
Chicken Tacos

*176*

Fiesta Casserole

Shrimp &
Andouille Sausage
Jambalaya

Blackened Salmon

Teriyaki
Pork Chops

Reuben Wraps

Slow Cooker
Cheesesteak
Pot Roast

# Side Dishes

Crispy Fried
Brussels Sprouts

Smashed Radishes

Roasted Cheesy
Cauli-Mac

Mushroom
Cauli-Risotto

Prosciutto
Provolone
Asparagus

Asiago Roasted
Green Beans

Cilantro Lime
Cauli-Rice

Spaghetti Squash
Fritters

Southern Summer
Squash Casserole

Sheet Pan
Parmesan Yellow
Squash & Zucchini

Roasted Garlic
Chive Cauli-Mash

# Desserts & Drinks

214 Zucchini Carrot Cake

216 Salted Dark Chocolate Almond Bark

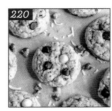
218 Lemon Cheesecake Mousse

220 Loaded N'oatmeal Cookies

222 Edible Cookie Dough

224 No-Bake Strawberry Cream Pie

226 German Chocolate Cake

228 Muddy Buddies

230 Peanut Butter Pie with Chocolate Crust

232 Skillet Blondie for Two

234 Peanut Butter Cup Bars

236 Lisa's Peanut Butter Cheesecake Brownies

238 Toasted Coconut Bars

240 Chocolate Cookie Crumbs

242 Dirt Cake

244 Magic Layer Bars

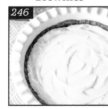
246 Banana Cream Pie

248 Toasted Coconut Custard

250 Red Velvet Cake

252 Forgotten Cookies

254 Strawberry-Infused Lemonade

256 Frosé

258 Sangria

260 Blackberry Mojito

262 Frozen Strawberry Margaritas

# Seasonings, Dressings & Other Basics

266
Blackening Seasoning

267
Ranch Seasoning

268
Ranch Dressing

269
Poppy Seed Dressing

270
Berry Vinaigrette

271
Roasted Tomato Marinara

272
Teriyaki Sauce

273
Buffalo Sauce

274
Sugar-Free Raspberry Jam

275
Sweetened Condensed Milk

276
Graham Cracker Crust

# ❧ General Index ❧